ADB THROUGH THE DECADES

ADB'S THIRD DECADE (1987–1996)

ASIAN DEVELOPMENT BANK

ADB

FOREWORD

The year 2016 marks the 50th anniversary of the Asian Development Bank (ADB). To commemorate this event, ADB has produced *ADB Through the Decades*, a series of volumes to provide a corporate chronicle over the past 5 decades of how ADB has evolved to engage its shareholders and other development partners in delivering financial and advisory services to its developing member countries in the Asia and Pacific region. Organized around key themes and topics for each decade, the series documents ADB's past work in such areas as strategic, operational, financial, and institutional developments.

The series synthesizes materials from many different sources, building from ADB's annual reports. The five volumes serve as decadal background notes for ADB's corporate history book, *Banking on the Future of Asia and the Pacific: 50 Years of the Asian Development Bank*, to be launched in 2017. Together, the history book and these volumes provide the first comprehensive corporate narrative on ADB's history since the previous ADB history book, *A Bank for Half the World*, was published in 1987.

Looking over the past 50 years, ADB has demonstrated a strong corporate continuity of being a multilateral development bank with an Asian character and global outreach. More significantly, the leadership of ADB has undertaken profound changes for the institution to stay relevant and responsive in serving the changing needs and expectations of its developing member countries. This spirit of change and innovation shall continue to drive ADB in the years ahead.

Reflecting on our history will give us a better insight for our work in the future. I hope that this *ADB Through the Decades* series becomes a key reference for ADB staff as well as other stakeholders from member countries, academic institutions, development partners, and civil society organizations.

TAKEHIKO NAKAO
December 2016

ACKNOWLEDGMENTS

This series, *ADB Through the Decades*, began as background research for the history book project chronicling the first 50 years of the Asian Development Bank (ADB). In the last 50 years, ADB has continuously evolved in response to dynamic changes across the Asia and Pacific region. The story of ADB's transformation became evident as the team tasked to support the ADB corporate history book project sifted through ADB's annual reports, past and present President's speeches, official and personal correspondences, loan documents, policy and strategy papers, evaluation reports, transcripts of interviews, historical records, and other archival materials. Drawing from the rich but fragmented sources of information, the team prepared background notes for each decade as an effort to capture and synthesize the significant developments and key turning points in ADB's history.

President Takehiko Nakao encouraged the team to publish the series as a stand-alone reference to a wider audience, including ADB staff. This work was done in parallel with the drafting of the ADB history book and took more than 2 years to complete. What were intended as internal supporting documents for the history book project in the end became five volumes that comprise the *ADB Through the Decades* series. This series provides the first comprehensive institutional record of the different facets of ADB's work—strategic, operational, financial, and organizational—spanning 50 years of ADB's history.

The first four volumes of the series were led by Valerie Hill, Director of the Strategy, Policy and Business Process Division (SPBP), Strategy, Policy and Review Department (SPD) with Edeena Pike, Strategy and Policy Specialist, Office of the Director General, SPD. The fifth volume was led by Ananya Basu, Principal Economist at the Pacific Department (PARD). Jade Tolentino, Research Consultant, provided substantive analytical support on all the volumes. Xianbin Yao, Director General, PARD, provided overall guidance and shared his insights on ADB's history to further enrich the notes. Peter McCawley, main author of the ADB history book, gave useful comments throughout the process.

This series benefited from comments and suggestions received from various departments and offices, as well as thematic and sector groups across ADB, during the interdepartmental review process. The volumes received written contributions from an interdepartmental focal group composed of Kinzang Wangdi (Budget, Personnel, and Management Systems Department [BPMSD]); Shanny Campbell and Noriko Sato (Central and West Asia Department); David Kruger (Department of External Relations [DER]); David Sobel (East Asia Department); Jesus Felipe and Juzhong Zhuang (Economic Research and Regional Cooperation Department [ERCD]); Medardo Abad, Jr. (Office of Administrative Services [OAS]); Nariman Mannapbekov (formerly of the Office of the Secretary [OSEC]); Emma Veve (Pacific Department [PARD]); Kiyoshi Taniguchi (Private Sector Operations Department [PSOD]) and Elsie Araneta (formerly of PSOD); Hiranya Mukhopadhyay (South Asia Department); Jason Rush (Southeast Asia Department); K. E. Seetharam (Sustainable Development and Climate Change Department [SDCC]) and Roshan Shahay (formerly of SDCC); and Mina Oh (Treasury Department [TD]).

Access to important historical records and data was vital in completing the *ADB Through the Decades* series. Technical inputs were provided by SPD (Vanessa Dimaano, Marvin de Asis, Socorro Regalado, and Grace Sevilla); Controller's Department (Setijo Boentaran and Lani Gomez); TD (Fean Asprer); BPMSD (Melanie dela Cruz and Kingzang Wangdi); and ERCD (Kaushal Joshi, Rana Hasan, Arturo Martinez, Pilipinas Quising, and Editha Lavina) in vetting the data used. The discussions on financial matters were largely drawn from the specialized report commissioned by TD on *A History of Financial Management at the Asian Development Bank*. Excellent support was extended by the OAS Records and Archives Unit (Medardo Abad, Jr., Richard Dimalanta, and Heidi Dizon) and Library Services (Marilyn Rosete and Voltere Serraon), who were always quick and resourceful in sourcing and screening historical photos and institutional documents; and OSEC (Nathaniel Casuncad, Genedyn Ebreo), who were ready to assist in Board document retrieval.

Overall production was supervised by Edeena Pike. DER (Robert Hugh Davis and Cynthia Hidalgo) helped in managing the volumes' production, particularly at the initial stages. Cherry Lynn Zafaralla was the copyeditor of the five volumes as well as publication coordinator. Joe Mark Ganaban provided the layout, graphics design, and typesetting, and Anthony Victoria of DER conceptualized the covers and box packaging design. Rowena Agripa, Lorena Catap, Esmeralda Fulgentes, Ma. Carolina Faustino-Chan, and Sharlene Guinto provided administrative assistance at various stages. Finally, the Logistics Management Unit of OAS (Razel Gonzaga and Wyn Lauzon) provided indispensable assistance in the printing of the volumes.

CONTENTS

TABLES, FIGURES, AND BOXES

ABBREVIATIONS

ADB	–	Asian Development Bank
ADF	–	Asian Development Fund
ASEAN	–	Association of Southeast Asian Nations
BOD	–	Board of Directors
DFI	–	development finance institution
DMC	–	developing member country
EDRC	–	Economics and Development Resource Center
GCI	–	general capital increase
ICT	–	information and communication technology
MTSF	–	medium-term strategy framework
NIE	–	newly industrializing economy
OCR	–	ordinary capital resources
ODA	–	official development assistance
PEO	–	Post-Evaluation Office
PRC	–	People's Republic of China
RETA	–	regional technical assistance
TA	–	technical assistance
WID	–	women in development

DATA NOTES

Lending approvals data used in the five volumes in this series, *ADB Through the Decades*, refer to loan, grant, equity investment, and guarantee approvals of the Asian Development Bank (ADB). They include sovereign and nonsovereign operations of ADB from 1967 to 2016. Approvals include ADB-funded lending operations from ordinary capital resources (OCR) and the Asian Development Fund. Cofinancing resources are discussed separately in the section "Financial Policies and Mobilization Efforts."

For both lending and technical assistance (TA) operations, regional breakdown is based on current member economy groupings of ADB. Central and West Asia includes Afghanistan, Armenia, Azerbaijan, Georgia, Kazakhstan, the Kyrgyz Republic, Pakistan, Tajikistan, Turkmenistan, and Uzbekistan. East Asia is composed of the People's Republic of China; Hong Kong, China; the Republic of Korea; Mongolia; and Taipei,China. South Asia covers Bangladesh, Bhutan, India, Maldives, Nepal, and Sri Lanka. Southeast Asia includes Brunei Darussalam, Cambodia, Indonesia, the Lao People's Democratic Republic, Malaysia, Myanmar, the Philippines, Singapore, Thailand, and Viet Nam. Finally, the Cook Islands, Fiji, Kiribati, the Marshall Islands, the Federated States of Micronesia, Nauru, Palau, Papua New Guinea, Solomon Islands, Timor-Leste, Tonga, Tuvalu, and Vanuatu comprise the Pacific developing member countries.

Lending data were sourced from two ADB databases, which use slightly different methodologies in recording project information. The operational approvals from 1967 to 1996 (volumes 1–3) were culled from the ADB loan, technical assistance, grant, and equity approvals database, which excludes terminated instruments (loans, grants, equity investments, and guarantees that were approved but terminated before their signing date). This database uses ADB's old sector classification system. Meanwhile, the operational approvals from 1997 to 2016 (volumes 4 and 5) were downloaded from ADB's Suite of Strategy 2020 Report of eOperations database which records gross approvals and follows a new project sector classification. All data are as of 31 December 2016.

Technical assistance operations data refer to TA approvals funded by the Technical Assistance Special Fund and Japan Special Fund only. For the first four volumes, the sources for the data are the loan, technical assistance, grant, and equity approvals database (as of 31 December 2016.); and for the fifth volume, ADB's Operations Planning and Coordination Division, Strategy, Policy and Review Department.

Staff information include management, international, and national and administrative staff. They include director's advisors and assistants, staff on special leave without pay, and on secondment status. Staff data are sourced from ADB's Budget, Personnel, and Management Systems Department, and may not tally with the numbers from ADB's annual reports, which used different classifications of staff data.

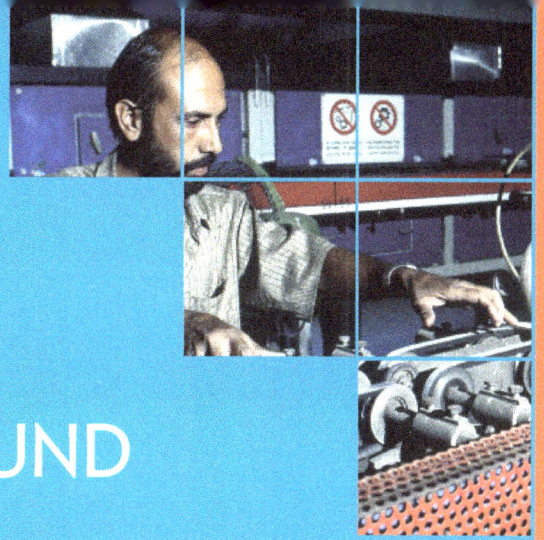

I. REGIONAL BACKGROUND

- Confidence in the region was growing during the third decade of the Asian Development Bank (ADB). Developing member countries (DMCs) drew more economic strength from within the region. There was much talk about the miracle of growth in Asia, just as the risks of a financial crisis were looming.
- By contrast, donor member countries were facing tight budgetary situations, and development assistance was getting more difficult to secure.

At the turn of the decade, economic reforms in the People's Republic of China (PRC) and India were beginning to bear fruit, and confidence in both Asian giants was beginning to grow. Confidence was growing in other parts of the region as well. Motivated by the sharp appreciation of the yen and following the Plaza Accord, Japanese industries moved their manufacturing industries into neighboring Asian countries. This pattern was replicated by the newly industrializing economies (NIEs), setting new flows of goods and capital within Asia and the Pacific. Other parts of the region also did well. In Southeast Asia, the end of regional conflict provided room for new policies, stability, and economic expansion. Across the Association of Southeast Asian Nations (ASEAN), a commitment to regionalism brought discipline to the reform process. Several ASEAN countries joined the international value chain of manufactured development through strong trade links with the PRC. As a whole, the region continued to grow (Table 1).[1] Toward the end of the third decade, there was much talk about the miracle of growth in Asia, just as the risks of financial crisis were looming.

In contrast, donor member countries were facing tight budgetary situations and development assistance was getting more difficult to secure, compared to the past. This situation affected all development institutions. Intense debate was taking place on different aspects of development assistance. These discussions generated some conclusions and broad consensus on certain issues. First, despite ongoing political and economic changes in the world, there continued to be a perceived need for development assistance and for an active role of

[1] See Appendix Tables A1.1 and A1.2 on selected economic and social indicators of the region.

international financial institutions in the process. Global challenges, such as those arising from environmental degradation, poverty, economic migration, and regional conflicts, required international cooperation, including well-directed development assistance. The challenge facing previously planned economies seeking transformation to market-based economic systems added a new dimension to this situation. Second, economic reforms had started to take hold in many developing countries. Support for their efforts by the major industrial countries and the multilateral institutions would, while meeting important development objectives, also contribute importantly to growth and employment in the industrial world. While international financial institutions were generally recognized as efficient channels for official development assistance, they were increasingly being called upon to demonstrate efficiency and effectiveness, in view of the difficult fiscal conditions in industrialized countries.

Table 1: Population and Gross Domestic Product, Selected Regional Groupings, 1966–2015

Regions	1966	1976	1986	1996	2006	2015
Developing Asia						
GDP ($ billion)	163	426	1,014	2,937	6,412	18,063
Population (million)	1,718	2,173	2,626	3,124	3,555	3,903
GDP per capita ($)	95	196	386	940	1,804	4,628
Share of world GDP (%)	8	7	7	9	13	25
Share of world population (%)	51	52	53	54	54	53
Asia's share of world GDP (constant, 2010 $) (%)	14	16	19	24	25	31
Latin America and Caribbean (excluding high-income economies)						
GDP ($ billion)	117	411	706	1,894	3,030	4,855
Population (million)	244	314	392	471	544	605
GDP per capita ($)	481	1,306	1,800	4,024	5,569	8,020
Share of world GDP (%)	6	6	5	6	6	7
Share of world population (%)	7	8	9	11	13	15
Sub-Saharan Africa (excluding high-income economies)						
GDP ($ billion)	42	142	235	348	798	1,571
Population (million)	264	342	454	600	783	1,001
GDP per capita ($)	158	416	518	581	1,019	1,570
Share of world GDP (%)	2	2	2	1	2	2
Share of world population (%)	8	8	9	10	12	14

GDP = gross domestic product.
Notes: Gross domestic product is expressed in current $ billion. Developing Asia includes developing member economies of ADB. Asia includes ADB's regional developing and developed members (Australia, Japan, and New Zealand).
Source: The World Bank. World Development Indicators. http://data.worldbank.org/indicator/NY.GDP.MKTP.CD (accessed 7 December 2016).

II. INSTITUTIONAL OVERVIEW

- Over the decade, ADB undertook major initiatives to transform itself from a project financier into a broad-based development institution.
- The expanding scope, diversity, and complexity of operations led to changes in ADB's strategic policy directions as well as its functions and organizational structure.

With the trends toward increased trade, investment, and cooperation, the development process had become increasingly complex. ADB adjusted over the years to respond to the new challenges. In its early years, ADB was primarily a project financier, focused on providing project lending to DMCs to create new productive capacity and support infrastructure designed to foster economic growth. The Bank did not initially concern itself overly with macroeconomic issues, as these were considered firmly within the jurisdiction of the Bretton Woods institutions. Responding to emerging needs, the Bank started in the second decade to expand its lending modalities and policy orientation by introducing program and sector loans. The Bank also gradually started to step up its lending for social infrastructure projects and more deliberately combined knowledge support with its lending, to establish itself as a "regional resource center." Over the third decade, ADB undertook major initiatives to transform itself into a broad-based development

institution able to coordinate closely with the World Bank and the International Monetary Fund, while maintaining a strong regional perspective and promoting and facilitating the mobilization of additional development resources for the region.

The decade started with a focus on strategy. An external panel of eminent development experts was commissioned to study the role of ADB in the 1990s,[2] which came out with a report that emphasized social infrastructure, living standards of the poorest groups, and protection of the environment as new priorities. A range of new policies and strategies were approved or updated throughout the decade. As donor expectations evolved, there was greater emphasis on effectiveness in the delivery of development assistance. ADB responded by strengthening its internal procedures and giving greater attention to project quality. Lending picked up considerably, with the PRC and India looking for more support while regional activities began

---

[2]   ADB. 1989. *The Asian Development Bank in the 1990s: Panel Report*. Manila.

to grow. New members such as Central Asian republics joined, and some existing but nonactive members renewed their regular links with ADB (Cambodia and Viet Nam). For the first time in 1994, ADB's lending program ran up against the lending headroom and had to be frozen. After some delay, the ceiling was relaxed and normal operations resumed. To centralize its operations, ADB moved to a new headquarters, as its activities had located to seven offices around Metro Manila over the years.

A.   Membership

Nine new members joined the Bank over the period. With the collapse of the former Soviet Union in December 1991, the Asia and Pacific region gained six independent states, three of which would become ADB members during the period: Kazakhstan and the Kyrgyz Republic (1994), and Uzbekistan (1995). Four Pacific

DMCs also joined: the Marshall Islands and the Federated States of Micronesia (1990), Nauru (1991), and Tuvalu (1993). The remaining new members were Mongolia and Turkey (1991). By the end of the third decade, ADB had 56 members (40 regional and 16 nonregional).

B.   Leadership

1.   Presidents

President Masao Fujioka resigned in 1989 upon reaching 65 years of age and after 8 years in office. His last day was on 23 November 1989.

On 12 September 1989, the ADB Board of Governors unanimously elected Kimimasa Tarumizu to succeed President Fujioka (see Box 1). President Tarumizu assumed office on 24 November 1989. He resigned in 1993, after 4 years in office, citing health reasons.

Box 1: Fifth ADB President Kimimasa Tarumizu
(24 November 1989–23 November 1993)

Kimimasa Tarumizu was 59 when he was appointed ADB's fifth President. A graduate of Tokyo University Faculty of Law, he joined Japan's Ministry of Finance in 1953, where he served for 32 years in various positions including Chief of Tokyo Customs and Senior Advisor to the Minister. Prior to joining ADB, he had wide experience in international finance including several overseas postings in London, New York, and Washington, DC.

President Tarumizu was consensus-minded. Under his leadership, interactions between the Board and Management increased, and Board members became more involved in important operational matters. ADB's annual lending commitments rose to almost $5 billion. One of his hallmarks was his concern for the "poorest of the poor." During his tenure, ADB redirected its financing activities toward more socially oriented development assistance programs. Regional cooperation was also given renewed emphasis, particularly with the establishment of the Bank's Greater Mekong Subregion Program. ADB formalized its strategic planning process and strengthened country programming. On the borrowing front, ADB entered new markets with the launch in 1991 of a $300 million "Dragon Bond" issue, which was offered simultaneously in the capital markets of Hong Kong, China; Singapore; and Taipei,China. President Tarumizu also oversaw the inauguration of ADB's new headquarters in Mandaluyong. He would also be credited for important improvements in staff policies, increasing transparency in recruitment and promotion, enhancement of training, and provision of opportunities to female staff.

President Tarumizu resigned from ADB in 1993 and passed away due to heart failure on 21 February 2009, in Japan, at the age of 78.

Sources: D. Wilson. 1987. *A Bank for Half the World: The Story of the Asian Development Bank*. Manila; other ADB sources.

In September 1993, the Board of Governors unanimously elected Mitsuo Sato to succeed President Tarumizu as ADB's sixth President (Box 2). President Sato assumed office in November 1993 and would serve until 1999.

2.   Vice-Presidents

There was significant rotation among the three Vice-President (VP) posts over the decade.[3] In 1987, the Board of Directors (BOD) reappointed Stanley Katz for a 2-year term as VP Finance and Administration, effective 1 April 1988. Just 4 months later, on 1 August 1988, In Yong Chung took over the post for a 5-year term, and Katz was redesignated as VP Operations, succeeding Narasimham who had resigned. Chung was Deputy Prime Minister and Minister of Economic Planning of the Republic of Korea from May 1987 to February 1988 and, prior to that, Minister of Finance (1986–1987). Katz would himself retire from the Bank in October 1990 and be replaced by William Thomson. Prior to his appointment as VP Operations, Thomson was the United States (US) Alternate Director on the Bank's Board of Directors. He had previously worked for 16 years in various capacities in the US Treasury Department. Thomson would resign from his position in June 1994 and be replaced by Peter Sullivan, who was also from the US and had been working for ADB since 1975. Prior to his VP appointment, he was ADB General Counsel.

Gunther Schulz was reappointed for a further 3-year term from 1 July 1989 and redesignated as VP Finance and Administration, succeeding In Yong Chung, who took over as VP Projects. Schulz would be reappointed for a further 3-year term beginning 1 July 1992. He would retire from ADB in June 1995 and be succeeded by Pierre Uhel. Prior to his appointment, Uhel (from France) was Executive Director at the African Development Bank representing Belgium, France, and Italy.

Box 2: Sixth ADB President Mitsuo Sato
(24 November 1993–15 January 1999)

With a career spanning more than 3 decades in Japan's Ministry of Finance, President Mitsuo Sato was considered an expert in international taxation. Born in 1933, he was a graduate of Tokyo University Faculty of Law. He joined the Ministry of Finance in 1955. In 1966, he completed a 1-year international program specializing in taxation in developing countries at Harvard Law School. From 1970 to 1973, he served overseas as Senior Economist in the Fiscal Affairs Department of the International Monetary Fund. He later served as a member of the Policy Board of the Bank of Japan and as Director General of the Customs and Tariff Bureau. Before joining ADB, he was Deputy President of the Tokyo Stock Exchange.

President Sato would lead the Bank through one of Asia's most challenging periods following the onset of the Asian financial crisis in 1997. During his tenure, ADB expanded its mandate significantly from being a project financier to a broad-based development finance institution, committed to pursuing social development objectives. President Sato oversaw the introduction and implementation of several financial policies and major policy reforms on good governance, gender equity, indigenous peoples, and working with nongovernment organizations. In times of widespread budgetary constraints, the President brought about satisfactory outcomes to the negotiations for ADB's fourth general capital increase and the sixth replenishment of the Asian Development Fund.

President Sato resigned from the Bank in 1999 for personal reasons. He died of heart failure in Tokyo on 20 October 2002, at the age of 69.

Sources: D. Wilson. 1987. *A Bank for Half the World: The Story of the Asian Development Bank*. Manila; other ADB sources.

---

[3]   The three Vice-President posts at the time were (i) VP Finance and Administration, responsible for financial, administrative, and other service functions; (ii) VP Operations, covering development policy, country economic, and general economic work, country programming, and central loan administration; and (iii) VP Projects, responsible for sector work and processing and implementation of loan and TA projects.

In 1993, Bong-Suh Lee was appointed as VP Projects to replace Chung. At the time of his appointment, Lee was an adviser to the Korea Institute for Industrial Economics and Trade, and the Korea Energy Economics Institute.

C. Budget, Staffing, and Other Organizational Matters

1. Budget

Owing to limited resources and a more cautious approach of the Bank, the internal administrative expenses budget grew modestly at an annual average of 8% over the third decade. This was less than the annual growth in the number of loan projects approved (9%) and much less than experienced in the previous decade.[4] By the end of 1996, actual internal administrative expenses amounted to $184 million, against an initial budget of $190 million and adjusted budget of $188 million. An integrated planning process linking the medium-term work program and the budget framework was introduced in 1991 (see section III.B.1).

2. Staffing and Human Resources Policy

By the end of the third decade, there were 1,961 ADB staff from 43 member countries, including 673 international and management staff and 1,288 local staff. This represented a 22% increase compared to the previous decade.[5] Along with the change in focus, the Bank's staffing requirements evolved. There was a gradual increase in emphasis given to economic planning and policy analysis skills as well as the

hiring of staff with interdisciplinary background. Women were also actively encouraged to apply for professional positions.[6]

In 1988, the Bank undertook a comprehensive study to estimate its future staffing requirements and developed a staff planning model (the STAFFPLAN model). To support its first Medium-Term Strategic Framework (MTSF),[7] the Bank presented its first human resource strategy paper in 1993. It would be finalized and adopted in 1996. The paper introduced a strategic planning and policy framework for key human resource management processes, including (i) recruitment and staffing, (ii) performance management, (iii) position classification, and (iv) professional staff salary and administration.

There was a strong emphasis on promoting staff learning and development, given the dynamic and constantly changing regional environment. Bankwide task forces were commissioned throughout the decade to review staff training and development activities, resulting in an action program that strengthened career planning and development. Training programs gave special attention to areas of increasing significance to ADB, including sector analysis and strategy development, good governance and capacity building, environment and social analyses, and policy analysis and reform. By the end of the decade, apart from in-house training, staff could also avail of external learning events, staff study tours, leave of absence for staff development, education assistance, temporary assignments within the institution, job rotation,[8] and computer-based self-learning programs. The External Assignment Program assigned selected staff to development agencies in DMCs. Meanwhile, to improve the skills of current and potential

---

[4] In the second decade, the Bank's internal administrative expenses budget grew at an annual average of 25% from 1977 to 1981 and 9% from 1982 to 1986, after the Budget Review Committee of the Board was established. By contrast, the number of loan projects grew at annual rate of just 3%.

[5] At the end of 1986, there were 1,604 staff from 37 member countries (599 international and management staff and 1,001 local staff).

[6] In 1990, in line with efforts to increase women's representation among professional staff, the Bank adopted a policy statement and action plan to promote the recruitment and career development of women professionals. An interdepartmental advisory committee on women professionals was established to assist in monitoring and implementing the policy.

[7] ADB. 1992. *The Bank's Medium-Term Strategic Framework, 1992–1995*. Manila.

[8] A job rotation scheme was introduced in 1988 to give high-potential staff exposure to different areas.

managers, the Manager Development Program was introduced in 1991. In 1993, the Professional Growth Promotion Guidelines were issued for operational job streams of professional staff. Similar guidelines were prepared for supporting staff. The Special Separation Program, approved in 1994, provided for the voluntary separation of staff. This improved staffing flexibility and provided better career opportunities for the remaining staff.

Staff compensation and benefit packages, including salary increase, insurance coverage, staff retirement plan, housing,[9] and education grant support,[10] were also reviewed regularly. In 1996, a comprehensive review of the professional staff salary policy and structure was completed. It recommended the continuation of a market-based approach for the determination of professional staff salary, using the World Bank wage structure as a benchmark. Further, revisions to the retirement plan were approved in 1996.[11]

In 1987, for the first time, a formal grievance procedure with an Appeals Committee was established, allowing staff to seek review of individual grievances concerning the terms and conditions of their employment. In 1990, a Personnel Handbook codifying the institution's personnel policies and practices was completed. The ADB Administrative Tribunal was set up in 1991 to serve as an independent external and impartial appeal mechanism for the resolution of employment disputes. Meanwhile, a major review of Professional Staff Performance Evaluation practices was undertaken in early 1992, introducing new rating classification and evaluation criteria for professional staff at different levels. In 1993, similar changes were introduced for supporting staff.

3.   Office Accommodation

After occupying its previous location on Roxas Boulevard for 19 years, ADB finally moved to its new headquarters in Mandaluyong in March 1991.[12] The new building was inaugurated by then Philippine President Corazon C. Aquino on 31 May 1991. The move allowed the Bank to centralize its operations, which had expanded to seven locations around Metro Manila. Sitting on a six-hectare site, the new headquarters consisted of a nine-story office block and a two-story facility block. Apart from office space, the building provided for a library, training center, communications center, computer center, auditorium, conference rooms, printing center, records center, cafeteria and dining room, telephone exchange, post office, commercial bank, and staff recreational facilities. The Bank would introduce several energy conservation measures in the building in the latter part of the decade.

4.   Resident Missions

In line with the greater emphasis on country focus and improving project quality, six new resident missions were opened in 1987 (Indonesia), 1989 (Nepal and Pakistan), 1992 (India), and 1996 (Cambodia and Viet Nam). In addition, three representative offices were established in donor countries to obtain a broader and more direct access to ADB's constituencies. The North American Representative Office opened in 1995 in Washington, DC to facilitate better communication with the governments of Canada and the US, and to liaise with their development communities, businesspersons, academe, and nongovernment organizations. The Japanese

---

[9]   In 1987, the staff housing loan program became operational.
[10] In 1993, the Bank revised the educational grant entitlement for both duty station and out-of-duty station schooling to reflect increases in the cost of education.
[11] The revisions included an increase in the pension accrual rate for pensioners who retired prior to 1987; the introduction of a dual-currency option for payment of pensions; and a change in the methodology for determining the conversion rate for the currency option.
[12] The new building was initially supposed to be completed by early 1988. Contractors were not able to meet the initial deadline.

Representative Office in Tokyo, Japan was opened in 1996 and would play an important role in strengthening ADB's resource mobilization efforts by promoting cofinancing with official and commercial sources. The third office, the European Representative Office in Frankfurt, Germany, opened in 1996 to enhance public awareness about ADB among its 14 European shareholders. By the end of 1996, there were 11 field offices worldwide (excluding the headquarters in Manila): seven resident missions,[13] one regional mission,[14] and three representative offices.

5.   Computerization

Through ADB's Office of Computer Services, progress was made in upgrading technologies and automating office processes to meet the expanding volume of operations. In 1987, new systems were implemented to facilitate onsite economic analysis of agriculture projects, monitor the status of internal Bank procurement activities, and administer borrowing transactions. In 1990, the mainframe computer data communications network was expanded. Other activities progressed in accordance with the 3-year (1989–1991) Computer and Office Automation Program approved by the Board. By 1992, expanded data communications network offered online mainframe access to about 1,800 terminals.

The Task Force on Information Technology (IT) Strategy was established in August 1991 to formulate a cost-effective IT strategy to support the Bank's mission and strategic objectives (up to the end of 1996) as outlined in the medium-term strategic framework. It provided for the implementation of cost-effective and efficient information and office automation systems; establishment and enhancement of an IT infrastructure to facilitate information flow; improvement of communication and coordination among departments; enhancement of operational capacity; and provision of effective end-user support in the proper and efficient use of computer systems. In 1994, network, Windows, and client-server-based platforms were implemented; and local area network servers, gateways, and a Bankwide electronic mail system were installed. By 1995, the ADB homepage, http://www.adb.org was launched, and the Lotus Notes infrastructure was completed. A review of the Information Systems Strategy was initiated in 1996, when work on the local area network was also completed.

---

[13]   The Bank opened its first resident mission on 20 July 1982 in Bangladesh.
[14]   The Board approved the opening of the Bank's South Pacific Regional Mission in Vanuatu in 1984.

6. Important Organizational Changes

The increase in scope, diversity, and complexity of the Bank's operations led to changes in its functions. Adjustments were made to the organizational structure. A major step toward regionalizing the Bank's operations came in 1987 with the establishment of six country-based divisions in the reorganized Agriculture Department. The Bank's Environment Unit, attached to the Office of the Director, Infrastructure Department, was established in 1987 to integrate environmental dimensions in the Bank operations. It was upgraded to a division in 1989, and subsequently elevated to the Office of the Environment in 1990. Likewise, a Private Sector Department was created to act as focal point for private sector activities within the Bank in 1989.

In 1991, a Strategic Planning Unit was created to assist Management in the strategic planning process, including formulation, implementation, monitoring, and evaluation of the medium-term strategic plan. This unit reported directly to the President, and was renamed the Strategy and Policy Office in 1994 when it was merged with the then Development Policy Office. It was created to assist Management in the strategic planning process, including formulation, implementation, monitoring, and evaluation of the medium-term strategic plan. The Infrastructure Department was also reorganized to establish country-based divisions. In 1992, a Social Dimensions Unit was established to integrate cross-cutting social dimensions into the Bank's operations.

A major internal reorganization was approved by the Board in 1994 to give ADB operations a sharper country focus and use resources more efficiently. The reorganization (which became effective on 1 January 1995) was based on broad geographic specialization (East and West) at the regional Vice-President level, functional specialization (programs and projects) at the department level, and technical specialization at the division level. Under the structure, VPs were in charge of all operating functions for countries under them. The central policy offices (including the Strategy and Policy Office, the Office of the Environment, and the Social Development Office) would report directly to the President. The functions of the VP Finance and Administration remained unchanged. The Office of Cofinancing Operations was established in 1996 to mainstream cofinancing activities in ADB operations. ADB's organizational structure at the end of the third decade is found on pages 62–63.

III. STRATEGIC DIRECTIONS AND OPERATIONAL AGENDA

- The decade started with a strong focus on strategy, which continued throughout. ADB formalized its strategic planning process and articulated a consolidated statement of corporate objectives over the medium term. A range of new policies and strategies were approved and/or updated.
- ADB more deliberately combined knowledge support with its lending to bolster its role as a broad-based development institution.

A. Review of the Bank's Role in the 1990s

At the Annual Meeting in 1987, several Governors called for a review of ADB's role in the 1990s. Consequently, an external panel was commissioned to assess the role and distinctive contribution that the Bank could make in response to the changing needs of its DMCs. The panel was chaired by the former Japanese foreign minister, Sabura Okita and included John M. Hennessy (former US Assistant Secretary for International Affairs); Emile van Lennep (former Secretary-General, Organisation for Economic Co-operation and Development); Mohammad Sadli (Indonesian policymaker and economist); and Amartya Sen (who would be awarded the Nobel prize for economics in 1998).

The Panel Report, *The Asian Development Bank in the 1990s*, was completed in January 1989.[15] Its recommendations covered a wide range of activities, and emphasized new strategic priorities and changes to ADB's operational agenda including (i) support for social infrastructure (especially public health and education); (ii) improvement of living standards of the poorest groups, with special attention to women; and (iii) protection of the environment. ADB's public sector support was to be reoriented in line with these new priorities. The Panel also recommended that the Bank take a more active role in helping to promote the private sector (directly or indirectly) and called for broader policy dialogue with DMCs.

The Panel proposed a number of operational modifications related to improvements in project

---

[15] ADB. 1989. *The Asian Development Bank in the 1990s: Panel Report.* Manila.

appraisal and implementation techniques; greater support in the field of population through public education and health projects; expansion and reorientation of technical assistance (TA) in support of the new priorities; review of ADF resources eligibility; more active participation in donor coordination activities; expansion of cofinancing activities; increased used of financial innovations; and the need to intensify efforts to foster regional cooperation. The Panel noted that the implementation of its recommendations would entail significant reorganization of the Bank's structure as well as strengthening of its staff.

B. Revised Operational Agenda

In line with the Panel recommendations, ADB adopted several measures to enhance its development role on one hand, and to improve the effectiveness and efficiency of its operations on the other.

1. Strengthening the Planning Process

The Bank established an internal task force in 1990 to assess its existing institutional arrangements for strategic planning. In its report completed in early 1991, the task force concluded that while the identification of strategic objectives and planning took place at a number of levels within the Bank, there was no coordination between activities, nor was there a consolidated statement of Bankwide objectives for the medium term. Management, therefore, established the Strategic Planning Unit in July 1991 to introduce a formal strategic planning system.[16]

The Strategic Planning Unit undertook three major steps to determine the Bank's program of operations: (i) articulation of development objectives which, while emphasizing economic growth, would increasingly address social concerns and environmental protection; (ii) adoption of a country focus in all aspects of operations; and (iii) planning steps that would facilitate translating the objectives and country focus into operational programs. A better linkage was also sought between the operational program and budget. In addition to the preparation of various country-focused documents (including country strategies and operational plans), the key features of the strategic planning process included the Medium-Term Strategic Framework (MTSF) paper; the Planning and Budget Directions by Management; and the Three-Year Rolling Work Program and Budget Framework, leading to the Bank's budget for the succeeding year. The BOD was closely involved in the process, through discussion of the 3-year rolling work program and the annual budget. This process is still in place to date.

In March 1992, the Bank adopted its first MTSF covering 1992–1995.[17] It defined five strategic objectives: (i) promotion of economic growth, (ii) reduction of poverty, (iii) improvement of the status of women, (iv) progress in population planning, and (v) promotion of sound management of natural resources and the environment. To achieve these objectives, the role of the private sector as well as efficient public sector management were emphasized. It also highlighted the Bank's mandate in fostering regional cooperation. The MTSF was updated annually, taking into account feedback from ongoing Bank operations, developments in the global and regional environment as well as DMCs' views. The MTSF, 1995–1998 replaced the objective of facilitating progress in population planning with a broader strategic objective of human development (including population planning).[18]

---

[16] The Strategic Planning Unit was created under the Office of the President in 1991. As part of ADB's broader reorganization in 1994, the unit was merged with ADB's Development Policy Office to become the Strategy and Policy Office, which was upgraded as the Strategy and Policy Department in 2000.

[17] ADB. 1992. *The Bank's Medium-Term Strategic Framework, 1992–1994.* Manila.

[18] ADB. 1994. *The Bank's Medium-Term Strategic Framework, 1995–1998.* Manila.

2. Broadening Operational Agenda

With the adoption of strategic planning, the Bank began to increase its attention to social concerns and environmental issues, and to do so in a more systematic way. As part of this effort, a new project classification system was introduced in 1992 to monitor the conformity of ADB lending programs with its broad development strategic objectives. At the same time, the Bank established a target that projects addressing cross-cutting concerns other than economic growth should account for at least 50% of the total number of loans. Such targets were considered necessary to build the Bank's capacity in these areas.

As an important element of the increased emphasis on strategic planning, all major sectors in which the Bank was involved were reviewed. Common issues were identified to ensure project success across sectors: (i) a DMC must have a conducive policy environment that includes the interaction of economywide and sector policies; (ii) the complementary and reinforcing role of public and private sectors must be strengthened; (iii) institutional capacity must be adequate to design and implement policy at the sector level and to implement projects at the executive agency level; and (iv) project viability must be ensured by adequate tariff levels and by providing for operation and maintenance expenditure in project design. Further, issues related to private sector development, public sector management, human resource development, and natural resource management should cut across all sectors and permeate all levels of operations. New policy areas emerged. Good governance linked to sound development management was articulated as a new policy. The Bank also actively started to work on promoting closer interaction among economies in the region in support of the regional cooperation agenda. Several steps were taken to improve operational practices and procedures. Organizational structure and staffing were also reviewed and adjusted.

3. Strengthening Economics and Research Work

In the beginning of the decade, the difficult international economic environment led DMCs to prioritize effective resource mobilization, efficient resource allocation, and investment activity. The Bank responded through intensified research programs and policy dialogue designed to assess and address the changing needs of DMCs. The Economics Office was renamed the Economics and Development Resource Center (EDRC), serving as the focal point for the Bank's economic and research work. Over the decade, EDRC sought to increase its involvement in ADB's operations and strengthen its role as a development resource center. To do so, EDRC worked more closely with the Project and Programs Departments to strengthen their macroeconomic and sector work. This included modification of macroeconomic models, development of economic evaluation guidelines, participation in country operational strategy studies, country programming and appraisal missions, and provision of sector studies. At the same time, it provided advisory TA in various areas, and served as resource persons at local, regional, and international conferences and seminars.

In-House Research and Special Studies. EDRC continued to undertake research on macroeconomic and microeconomic aspects of development, covering the following topics: regional cooperation (e.g., growth triangles); agriculture policies (rice market, revitalization of rural Southeast Asia, fertilizer subsidies, rural credit delivery systems, commodity price projections); international economics (foreign trade barriers, regional cooperation, trade in services); public finance (public sector development expenditure); macroeconomic policies (East Asian economic development, exchange rate policies and financial sector issues, impact of the integration of the European Economic Community on DMCs, international capital flow and external debt issues, foreign direct investments, demographic–economic forecasting); and special topics in development economics (economic consequences of aging, population growth and distribution, urbanization and the environment, HIV/AIDS). Sector-oriented research included project-related issues such as the estimation of shadow pricing for project approval; disease impact assessment; economic analysis of education and water supply projects; and estimation of the poverty alleviation impact of agricultural projects. Country- and region-specific research was also undertaken, and an active TA program was maintained to assist DMCs in the development and strengthening of statistical systems and services, with increasing priority accorded to strategic areas such as poverty reduction, the environment, women in development, and social development.

Other Operational Support. EDRC also oversaw the economic evaluation of loan and TA activities, participating in the appraisal process of new loans and TA projects and in their evaluation upon completion. In line with the recommendations of the Task Force on Improving Project Quality (see section V.B), new *Guidelines for Economic Analysis of Projects* were issued in 1996. The *Guidelines for Economic Analysis of Telecommunications Projects* were also prepared, and work was begun on guidelines for economic analysis of urban development projects, benefit measurements for rural electrification, and best practice studies for power projects. A Board information paper on Bank criteria for subsidies was also prepared.

Strengthening of Statistical System. In 1990, EDRC began work on a computer-based statistical data bank, consolidating socioeconomic data on DMCs for use by the Bank and its member countries. The database became operational in 1992. ADB collaborated closely with other international organizations to facilitate exchange of statistical data. By 1996, the Statistics and Data System Division (EDSD) homepage became accessible to provide statistical data to both staff

and external users. Regional TA projects were undertaken to compile and disseminate social, environment, and gender indicators. TA was also provided to strengthen national statistical systems in DMCs, particularly in the transitional economies and those in the South Pacific.

Dissemination, Outreach, and Capacity Building. The Bank continued to disseminate its research findings through its research monograph series: *Economic Staff Papers, EDRC Report Series, EDRC Occasional Paper Series, EDRC Technical Note Series,* and *EDRC Statistical Report Series* (all of which would be consolidated a decade later into one series, the *ADB Economics Working Paper Series*). The center also produced the *EDRC Policy Brief Series* for Management; as well as the Bank's only policy journal, the *Asian Development Review*; and ADB's annual flagship statistical publication, *Key Indicators of Developing Asian and Pacific Countries.* A number of new publications were also introduced, most notably the *Asian Development Outlook,* which provides a broad view of economic progress in the DMCs. EDRC also maintained its active involvement in human resource development in the region. The development of economic analysis and provision of training to DMC officials were promoted through programs in selected DMCs. Technical assistance was provided for statistical training; development of national accounts; and training in macroeconomic management, taxation, and financial policies. The Bank partnered with other development institutions such as the Asian Productivity Organization, the Association of Development Research and Training Institutes of Asia and the Pacific, and the International Monetary Fund to support these learning activities for DMC government officials. Conferences, seminars, and roundtable discussions were held on various economic issues with intensified collaboration with national, regional, and international institutions. The Annual Conference on Development Economics was started in 1992 and served as a forum for the discussion of cutting-edge research and thinking.

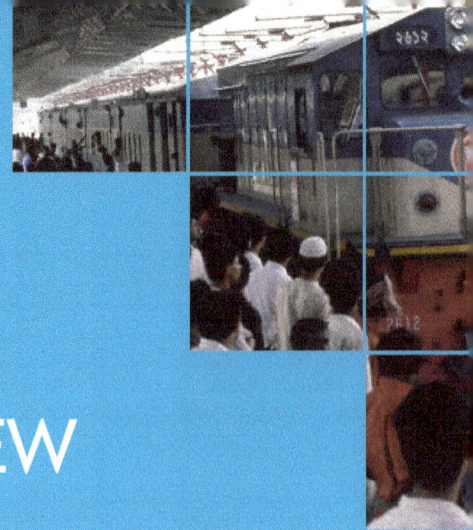

IV. OPERATIONAL OVERVIEW

- The People's Republic of China and India became active borrowers as lending operations continued to expand and regional activities began to grow.
- Over the decade, ADB reviewed and adjusted its approach in a number of key sectors and thematic priorities in response to changing circumstances. While energy and transport still accounted for the bulk of total lending, ADB started to increase its attention to social concerns and environmental issues.
- The Bank also increased its focus on policy dialogue and reforms.

A. Lending Overview

Lending operations continued to expand in the third decade, reaching $43 billion, an almost threefold increase from the second decade, with 30% of lending financed from ADF. Public sector and government-guaranteed loans accounted for 96%, with the rest going to direct private sector loans or equity. Annual lending commitments grew at an average of 14% from 1987 to 1993 before dropping by 29% in 1994. The decline was due to a combination of factors. First, difficult negotiations for a new general capital increase (GCI IV) took over 8 years to complete. As a result and for the first time, ADB's lending program hit the lending headroom in 1994. At the same time, in response to the recommendations of the Task Force on Improving Project Quality,[19] ADB undertook a one-time spring cleaning of its portfolio

to weed out inactive and slow-moving projects, and implemented a freeze on new lending activities. The Bank used this opportunity to conduct a deeper examination of the absorptive capacity of some of its borrowers. Normal lending resumed in 1995 and 1996, back to 1992–1993 levels and above the $5 billion annual mark (Figure 1).

B. Geographic Distribution

Compared to the previous decade, the geographic distribution of ADB lending shifted, as the PRC and India became active borrowers (each accounting for 15% of total lending over the decade). Consequently, the share of lending going to South Asia and East Asia increased. Southeast Asia continued to receive the greatest share, though its share was reduced from 52% in the second

---

[19] ADB. 1994. *Report of the Task Force on Improving Project Quality*. Manila.

Figure 1: Lending Operations by Fund Type, 1987–1996
($ million)

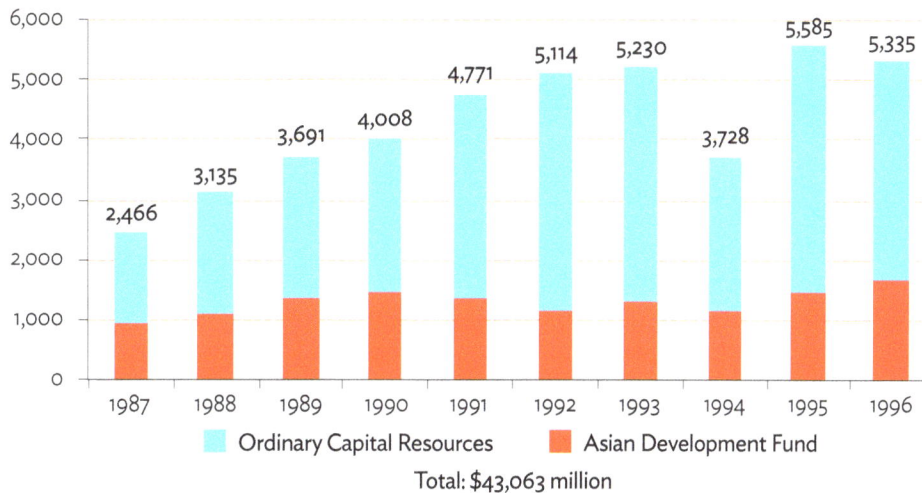

2,466   3,135   3,691   4,008   4,771   5,114   5,230   3,728   5,585   5,335

1987   1988   1989   1990   1991   1992   1993   1994   1995   1996

■ Ordinary Capital Resources   ■ Asian Development Fund

Total: $43,063 million

Note: Lending operations include loan, grant, equity investment, and guarantee approvals.
Source: ADB loan, technical assistance, grant, and equity approvals database.

decade to 41% in the third. Lending to Indonesia increased significantly, accounting for more than half of lending to Southeast Asia. ADB resumed lending to Cambodia and Viet Nam after a hiatus of almost 2 decades.[20] The share of lending to Central and West Asia declined modestly from 18% in the second decade (1977–1986) to 14% in the succeeding 10 years (1987–1996). ADB new members (Kazakhstan, the Kyrgyz Republic, and Uzbekistan) borrowed for the first time only in the latter part of the decade. Afghanistan stopped borrowing in 1979 and would not resume activities until 2001, due to political factors. The Pacific subregion continued to account for the smallest share of lending, with Papua New Guinea accounting for more than half of lending to the Pacific. The top five borrowers over the third decade were Indonesia (22%), the PRC (15%), India (15%), Pakistan (13%), and the Philippines (9%). Figure 2 shows lending operations by region.

Figure 2: Lending Operations by Region, 1987–1996
($ million)

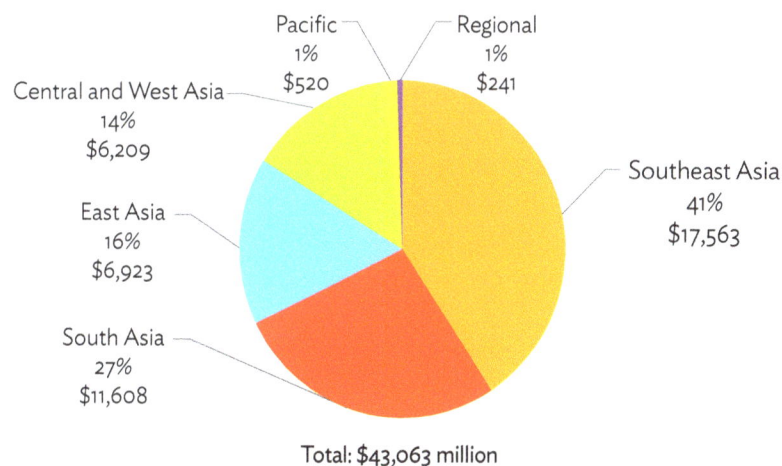

Pacific
1%
$520

Regional
1%
$241

Central and West Asia
14%
$6,209

Southeast Asia
41%
$17,563

East Asia
16%
$6,923

South Asia
27%
$11,608

Total: $43,063 million

Notes: Regional breakdown is based on current country groupings of ADB. Lending operations include loan, grant, equity investment, and guarantee approvals.
Source: ADB loan, technical assistance, grant, and equity approvals database.

[20] Viet Nam received no loans from 1975 to 1992. Cambodia did not borrow from 1971 to 1991. ADB resumed operations in Cambodia in 1991 after the Paris Peace Accord. ADB lending resumed in Viet Nam in 1992 when the US embargo was lifted. See R. Wihtol. 1988. *The Asian Development Bank and Rural Development: Policy and Practice*. Hampshire: Macmillan Press. p.102.

1. The People's Republic of China: Start of Operations

ADB's operations in the PRC started in 1986, at a time when the country was in the process of moving rapidly from a centrally planned economy to a market-oriented system. During the first 10 years of operation (1986–1996), ADB lending in the PRC reached $6.3 billion. All loans were financed from ordinary capital resources (OCR). Lending was heavily concentrated on physical infrastructure with transport and information and communication technology (ICT) accounting for 41% of lending, and the energy sector accounting for another 22%. The Bank's lending operations were complemented by its TA operations, which amounted to about $100 million over the same period. The Bank's TA assisted the PRC in preparing projects, instituting policy reforms, and supporting institution building. The PRC's lack of access to ADF limited the Bank from playing a key role in addressing social development issues and issues that were at the core of the Bank's new MTSF. However, there was a significant evolution in the composition and location of the Bank's PRC portfolio over the decade.

The first half of the decade (1986–1991) was a formative stage in the relationship between the Bank and the PRC. During this period, the PRC borrowed mainly for its industries either directly or through financial intermediaries. ADB operations were largely in the eastern coastal seaboard, which was the country's economic heartland, chosen by the PRC government to be developed as a growth corridor for the whole country. During this period, the Bank played a minor role in identifying projects to finance. It was, by and large, the central authorities who decided which projects were to be funded. The second phase (1992–1996) coincided with significant reforms and economic development following Deng Xiaoping's southern tour. ADB operations grew rapidly. As a result of continuous dialogue with the government on the Bank's desire to diversify its operational program to cover more energy and infrastructure projects, the government allowed provincial governments with

adequate foreign exchange repayment capacity to borrow from ADB for selected infrastructure projects. This led to a major shift in the portfolio from industry and finance to infrastructure. Apart from infrastructure, there was substantial lending for the financial sector and environment-related projects mostly in the industry sector. There were also increased efforts toward making cofinancing arrangements with the private sector. By the end of the decade, ADB's concern about poverty reduction was better understood, which led to a shift in regional focus into the poorer interior provinces.[21]

2. India: Start of Operations

After opting to be a nonborrowing member for 2 decades, India decided to borrow from ADB starting in 1986, mainly to access an additional (although modest in the country context) source of external finance. The first two country operational strategy studies approved in 1986 and 1990 supported the Government of India's strategic thrust of developing a modern, technologically progressive economy. From 1986 to 1996, ADB lending reached $6.6 billion and was primarily oriented to support the government program of industrialization through loans to state-owned financial intermediaries and public infrastructure development (power, roads, railways, ports). Projects in the energy and transport sectors accounted for almost three-fourths (73%) of total lending. The rest went to finance (16%), public sector management (4%), multisector (4%), industry and trade (2%), and water and other municipal infrastructure services (2%). All loans were financed from OCR. Unavailability of ADF support precluded ADB assistance to the agriculture and social sectors. Lending operations were supported by TA, which amounted to $35 million over the period.

Although ADB's assistance clearly helped to alleviate infrastructure bottlenecks, links to reforms and policy dialogue were weak for a number of reasons: (i) ADB had just started operations in India and was still getting to know the borrower, the sectors, and their issues—which was reflected in the still relatively low number of projects; (ii) ADB wanted its emerging relationship with India to be supportive rather than confrontational; and (iii) the political environment at the time was not conducive to externally driven policy dialogue. Several sector studies examining policy issues were launched and ADB staff gradually engaged in policy dialogue at the sector level.

After India started to introduce policy reforms in 1991, there was greater scope to translate sector policy dialogue into lending programs. The government played a major role in designing the reform measures. ADB responded by broadening its operational focus to include institutional and policy support. ADB's swift response to India's balance of payment crisis in 1991 through the Financial Sector Program Loan supported the government's wide-ranging sector reforms. Subsequent country strategy (approved in 1996) would emphasize support for financial sector restructuring and the development of policy, regulatory, and institutional frameworks in ADB's assistance for infrastructure development. It would also shift the focus from central government entities to state governments (Box 3). ADB's quick response to the crisis and its shift to state-level operations, particularly in the northeastern and other poorer states, strengthened relations between ADB and the Government of India. The government came to regard ADB as a valuable, responsive development partner, which enabled ADB to begin to address policy issues more proactively through program loans as well as project assistance.[22]

3. Focus on Transition Economies

Several DMCs were considered economies in transition at the time: Cambodia, the PRC, the Lao People's Democratic Republic (Lao PDR), Mongolia, Myanmar, and Viet Nam; as well as three republics of the former Soviet Union (Kazakhstan, the Kyrgyz Republic, and Uzbekistan). ADB's operational strategy in those countries centered on

three types of assistance: (i) short-term assistance to help their economies survive the shock of restructuring; (ii) financing for development of infrastructure, capital equipment, and technology to raise efficiency and environmental standards; and (iii) policy advice to build market-supporting institutions. ADB provided this assistance with a mix of program and project loans, and TA grants. ADB worked in close collaboration with the World Bank and the International Monetary Fund, which were providing policy advice related to macroeconomic stabilization and structural adjustment programs. ADB also collaborated closely with the European Bank for Reconstruction and Development, the United Nations Development Programme, and a number of bilateral donors. ADB assistance was accompanied by policy advice and sector restructuring to ensure better governance and appropriate macroeconomic and sectoral policies.

Short-term assistance included agriculture sector program loans to Kazakhstan, the Kyrgyz Republic, Mongolia, and Viet Nam. Policy advice focused on institutional reform, promotion of competitive markets, improvement of agricultural infrastructure, facilitation of restructuring, privatization of state-owned enterprises, and social and environmental concerns. Loans to the industrial sector supported policy and institutional reforms, private sector development, and strengthening of the legal and regulatory framework. Loans for infrastructure improvement included construction of expressways in the PRC, rural infrastructure improvement in Cambodia, and integrated urban development in the Lao PDR. By alleviating constraints in key sectors and supporting key policy reforms, ADB sought to improve economic efficiency and growth while at the same time addressing environmental concerns. ADB also conducted research and TA activities to help countries understand the transition process and its associated problems. ADB financed projects for capacity building and institutional development (for legal reforms, capital market development, and banking sector reforms) and to promote regional cooperation.[23]

22 ADB. 2007. *Country Assistance Program Evaluation for India*. Manila.
23 ADB. 1996. *Annual Report 1995*. Manila. pp.19–39.

Box 3: The Beginnings of State-Level Lending in India

Economic liberalization, coupled with an expansionist fiscal stance of the Government of India in the late 1980s, accelerated the country's economic growth. However, it also led to widening fiscal deficits. The fiscal imbalance spilled over into the balance of payments, and the sharp increase in oil prices caused by the Gulf crisis (1990–1991) triggered an economic crisis in India. National transfers to the states continued to decrease, and the government allowed reform-oriented states to negotiate loans from multilateral institutions.

Around the same time, Asian Development Bank (ADB) was in the process of revising its country operational strategy (COS) for India, and agreed, for the first time, to support state governments. The COS (completed in 1996) outlined a strategy for state-level public resource management reforms, which focused on three areas: fiscal consolidation, state-owned enterprise (SOE) reform, and enabling of private sector participation. During the COS formulation, an ADB mission visited Gujarat, Maharashtra, Punjab, and Tamil Nadu to identify potential states for ADB support. Gujarat was the first to be selected; a decision influenced by the fact that in 1992 the Gujarat state government had already constituted the Gujarat State Finance Commission, which released a set of recommendations in 1994 on how to address its deteriorating fiscal condition. ADB thus started a partnership with Gujarat, a progressive and reform-oriented state with a culture of market orientation, private entrepreneurship, and tradition of good administration and governance.

Being the first state-level public sector resource management loan, two factors characterized the formulation of the Gujarat Public Sector Resource Management Program. First, the program was designed by ADB staff in conjunction with Gujarat state government officials, drawing largely on the recommendations of the Gujarat State Finance Commission. Second, it was completed over a relatively short time—9 months from reconnaissance to loan agreement. The ADB Board eventually approved a $250 million loan for the program in December 1996. This marked the beginning of a strategic shift in ADB operations for India toward active state-level operations. The program was expected to (i) strengthen state finances and their prudent management, (ii) reform SOEs contributing to the state economy, and (iii) encourage private sector participation in infrastructure development in the state.

This was the first program loan provided by any multilateral development bank to a subnational government in India (or any ADB developing member country). ADB was to lead the way in directly supporting state fiscal adjustment and structural reforms to be complemented by sector support (in energy, roads, railways, ports, and telecommunications) emphasizing private sector participation. Through succeeding decades, ADB would follow with similar loans in Madhya Pradesh (1999), Kerala (2002), Assam (2004 and 2008), Mizoram (2009), and West Bengal (2012). Other development partners would follow ADB's lead in targeting assistance to states. An independent evaluation of ADB's program in India concluded that the strategic shift from central to state-level operations helped improve the geographic and institutional focus of ADB's country program to India, which, together with comparatively high sector selectivity, facilitated a more efficient and effective use of ADB's resources. It was also seen as being instrumental to improving relations between ADB and the Government of India.

Sources: ADB. 2007. *Country Assistance Program Evaluation for India.* Manila; ADB. 2007. *Project Performance Evaluation Report on India: Gujarat Public Sector Resource Management Program.* Manila; ADB South Asia Department.

C. Sectoral Developments

Energy and transport accounted for half of total lending over the decade, followed by agriculture (16%), finance (11%), water[24] (8%), education and industry (5% each), health and multisector (2% each), and public sector management (1%) (Figure 3). Over the decade, ADB adjusted its approach in a number of key sectors, in response to changing circumstances.

1. Energy

ADB lending to the energy sector reached over $11 billion (a 176% increase compared to the previous decade), overtaking agriculture and making it the largest sector, accounting for 26% of total lending. The bulk of assistance went to the power subsector. Around 34% of total energy loans went to electricity transmission and distribution, 28% to conventional energy, 15% to

---

[24] Includes other municipal infrastructure and services.

Figure 3: Lending Operations by Sector, 1987–1996
($ million)

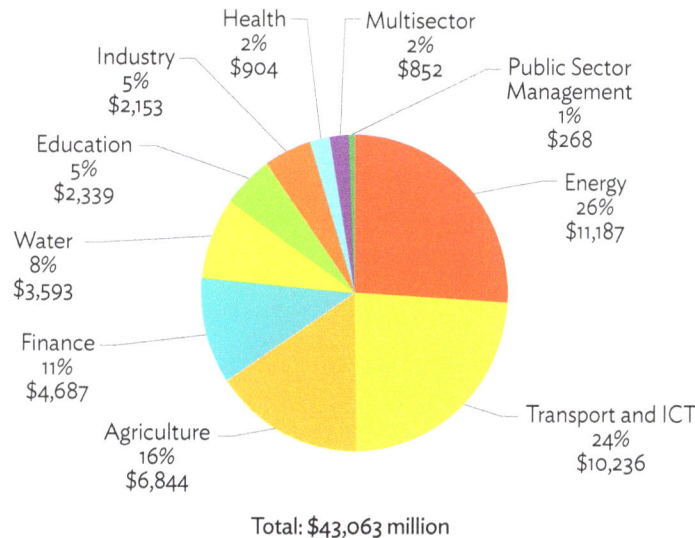

Total: $43,063 million

ICT = information and communication technology.
Note: Lending operations include loan, grant, equity investment, and guarantee approvals.
Source: ADB loan, technical assistance, grant, and equity approvals database.

large hydropower, and 13% to energy sector development. The remaining assistance was shared by energy efficiency and conservation (a new area of focus in the third decade accounting for 5% of total sector lending), pipelines (4%), and renewable energy (1%). Around 86% of energy loans were financed from OCR. The top five borrowers were India (25%), Indonesia (19%), Pakistan (14%), the PRC (13%), and the Philippines (10%).

The rising demand for energy loans reflected the steady increase in energy and electricity consumption. Yet the region's per capita consumption remained relatively small, compared with the rest of the world. ADB operations continued to focus on promoting cost-effective fuel diversification and substitution of indigenous and renewable energy forms of oil. Increasing financial demands inspired the development of innovative funding strategies, such as the build–operate–transfer and build–operate–own schemes. In 1989, for the first time, the Bank financed a private sector project for power generation (in the Philippines). This build–operate–transfer project included the Bank's first equity investment in the energy sector.[25]

ADB also used program and sector loans to try to correct energy price distortions, enhance energy efficiency, strengthen the institutional framework, and increase private sector participation. The Bank continued to attract cofinancing resources for energy development projects. Box 4 provides a synthesis of postevaluation in the power subsector.

Environmental considerations were given more prominence, especially in the second half of the decade. In 1996, the Bank approved a loan for renewable energy in India (Box 5). ADB expanded its lending portfolio to projects related to energy efficiency and conservation (to address capacity constraints), conventional and nonconventional energy resources development, and intensified environmental initiatives. ADB sought to help DMCs enhance the efficiency of their energy delivery networks, cut losses in distribution, and upgrade maintenance and operations of facilities. To meet these goals, the Bank continued to promote least-cost planning, construction and operation of energy systems, pricing reforms, and measures to make energy utilities operationally autonomous and financially viable.

[25] ADB. 1989. *Report and Recommendation of the President to the Board of Directors: Proposed Loan—Hopewell Energy (Philippines)*. Manila (Loan 7043/0991).

Box 4: Synthesis of Postevaluation Findings in the Power Subsector

The power sector was the largest recipient of Bank assistance from 1967 to 1996, comprising about 20% of the total value of bank lending (or $12.5 billion). ADB sought to (i) expand or upgrade power supply to meet growing demand for electricity, (ii) reduce dependence on imported oil for energy needs, (iii) improve overall power systems reliability and efficiency, and (iv) improve access of the poor to electricity. Overall, 79% of postevaluated projects in the sector were found to be generally successful, 20% were partially successful, and 1% was unsuccessful. ADB's experience highlighted the following lessons.

- **Tariffs reforms**. The financial viability of power utilities depended largely on how electricity tariffs were managed. Tariffs levels were found to be generally too low and their structures too complicated. Yet, many DMC governments were reluctant to approve tariff increases. Tariff reforms require full government support. Electricity prices should reflect the true economic costs involved.

- **Timely and adequate operation and maintenance**. The reliability of power supply and sustainability of project benefits were contingent on the operation and upkeep of project facilities. In some DMCs, governments were more concerned with obtaining new generating equipment than properly maintaining existing equipment. Operations and maintenance problems were often attributed to nonavailability of spare parts, lack of technical personnel, and inadequacy of budgetary allocations.

- **Reduction of system losses.** The single most important operational challenge facing many power utilities was the reduction of system losses. In a number of projects, loss reduction programs were implemented usually involving progressive metering of all electricity consumers, recertification of energy meters, resealing and rehabilitation of service terminals, and enactment and revision of electricity legislation to enforce accountability and curb illegal practices.

- **Shortage of qualified personnel.** Difficulties in recruiting and retaining suitable technical and managerial personnel were identified as major causes of institutional weakness. Regular training programs could help to ensure continuous availability of capable personnel. A greater degree of autonomy for executing agencies to determine staff remuneration would allow compensation to move toward market levels, allowing them to compete for qualified technical personnel.

- **Institutional strengthening and capacity building.** Bank assistance for the establishment and institutional support of strategic planning units in power utility companies would allow them to identify clear and achievable objectives, and conduct technical assessments of resources and options. ADB assistance for such institutional support in power projects in Thailand were mentioned as excellent examples of successful institution strengthening and capacity building components.

- **Environmental control.** The environmental and health impacts of power plants in some DMCs necessitated adopting mitigative measures in the design of these plants to (i) conserve and manage ecological systems, (ii) control pollutants and wastes, and (iii) protect public health.

- **Private sector participation in power provision.** The integration of independent power producers was often proposed as a supply-side solution to achieve optimal utilization of generating capacities, greater power availability, and lower systems costs. However, in some cases, it complicated the management and reduced the economies of scale in power operations. Governments should carefully weigh the benefits and costs of allowing greater private sector participation in power generation compared with having the public sector provide power and improving their efficiency instead.

Source: ADB. 1997. *Sector Synthesis of Post-evaluation Findings in the Power Subsector*. Manila.

Box 5: ADB's Renewable Energy Loan in India

The Asian Development Bank (ADB) implemented a $100 million loan (approved in late 1996) to support the Government of India's plan for expanding the development of four major technologies for renewable energy sources (RES): biomethanation for production of energy, bagasse-based cogeneration of power, wind energy development, and solar-thermal systems; and for facilitating the transition of RES technologies to mainstream status.

By supporting the development of RES, of which India had substantial potential, ADB support would contribute to addressing India's power shortages, reducing the energy sector dependence on fossil fuel, developing an environmentally friendly energy supply through renewable sources, and preventing depletion of India's limited resources including forests. The project would tap financial and managerial resources from the private sector and help promote environmentally sound investments in small-scale power generation using RES technologies. The loan, onlent to private entrepreneurs at commercial terms, would facilitate the generation of about 125 megawatts equivalent, which would reduce coal consumption in the country by about 625,000 tons per year. Provisions were made for capacity building of the institutions tasked with promoting and financing RES technologies in India. The loan was supposed to serve as a model for replication in other developing member countries in formulating appropriate regulatory and institutional framework, as well as designing an economically, financially, and technically viable program for RES development.

Source: ADB. 1996. *Report and Recommendation of the President to the Board of Directors: Proposed Loan and Technical Assistant Grant to the Indian Renewable Energy Development Agency, Limited for the Renewable Energy Development Project.* Manila (Loan 1465).

A new energy sector policy paper was approved in 1995.[26] The policy focused on increasing private sector participation in large-scale energy investments; improving energy efficiency (on both supply and demand sides), and further integrating environmental considerations in energy development. ADB would encourage power utilities to incorporate in their planning model key elements of integrated resource planning, including demand-side management and internalization of environmental costs. DMCs would also be encouraged to phase out subsidies to the power subsector and minimize cross-subsidies. In the hydrocarbon subsector, ADB would fund the development, processing, transportation, and distribution of natural gas. It would actively promote environmentally sound coal mining practices and clean coal technologies. Providing commercial energy in rural areas would receive priority (if economically and financially viable). Technical assistance would be provided to assess the financial viability of solar, minihydro, and wind energy options, particularly in isolated rural locations.

2. Transport and Information and Communication Technology

Primarily sourced from OCR resources, operations in the transport and ICT sector reached $10.2 billion over the decade (an increase of more than fivefold compared to the previous decade), as considerable investments were required to expand and improve transport and communication facilities. The sector's share of lending doubled from 12% in the second decade to 24% in the third decade, making it the second largest sector after energy. ADB operations in the sector remained heavily focused on roads (65%), followed by ICT and rail (12% each), water transport subsector (9%), and air transport (2%). Compared to the previous decade, ADB placed greater emphasis on developing the ICT sector. In contrast, the share of sector lending going to water transport decreased from 26% in previous decade to just 9% in the current decade. The top five country recipients were the PRC (26%), India (18%), Indonesia (15%), Thailand (9%), and Bangladesh (8%).

---

[26] ADB. 1995. *Bank Policy Initiatives for the Energy Sector.* Manila.

Transport operations focused on operational efficiency and environmental pollution control. In the road subsector, ADB emphasized (i) upgrading existing roads, improving their maintenance, and constructing new ones, while ensuring the availability of funds needed for these activities; (ii) imposing adequate user charges; and (iii) encouraging efficiency by liberalizing road transport policies and deregulating transport industry operations to facilitate entry. Various mechanisms were used to encourage private sector participation, including build–operate–transfer and build–operate–own arrangements. Railway and port systems were upgraded and modernized to increase their capacity and productivity. Commercial management practices were encouraged to facilitate operational efficiency. The priority in urban transport was to (i) provide key infrastructure to remove congestion and promote economic growth, (ii) maximize efficiency through improved traffic management, (iii) develop efficient public transport systems, and (iv) enhance the capacity of sector operators through institutional strengthening and human resources development. Airports were upgraded on a selective basis, with emphasis given to safety aspects.

Telecommunications were also increasingly considered as essential to a country's economic development and competitiveness. In 1993, ADB adopted a new telecommunication strategy that emphasized (i) modernizing telecommunications networks; (ii) improving operational efficiency and quality of service; (iii) gradually commercializing operations and introducing private ownership; (iv) strengthening policy, regulatory, and institutional aspects; (v) promoting a stronger commercial, financial, and managerial focus of government-operated companies; (vi) removing distortions in costing and pricing; (vii) mobilizing resources for sector development, including the promotion of private sector investment; and (vii) strengthening sector institutions, particularly planning, regulation, and human resources development.[27] While the primary focus on supporting economic growth remained, projects were to be selected, whenever possible, with a view to improving

access of disadvantaged groups in low-income, rural, and remote areas so as to promote balanced regional development.

3.   Agriculture

The share of the agriculture sector in the Bank's total lending fell significantly from 31% in the second decade to just 16% in the third decade, with the decrease being more pronounced in the second half (1992–1996). The decline was due partly to conscious reductions in the number of loans for the sake of quality (given the complex social and environmental objectives involved); partly to allow more equal sector distribution of country programs; and partly to unanticipated country constraints (i.e., India opted not to borrow for agriculture, and the PRC only borrowed a very limited amount). About two-thirds of agriculture loans were concentrated in irrigation, drainage, and flood protection (34%); and agriculture, production, and markets (30%). The rest went to forestry (10%); land-based natural resources management (9%); agriculture and rural sector development (6%); fishery (5%); water-based natural resources management (4%); and livestock (1%). The majority of loans (62%) were sourced from ADF. The top five country recipients were Indonesia (28%); Pakistan (22%); Bangladesh (10%); the Philippines (10%); and the PRC (6%). Box 6 summarizes postevaluation findings in the irrigation and rural development sector.

The Bank reoriented its approach to the agriculture sector in the second half of the decade.[28] ADB new directions emphasized (i) resource management and sustainable development with particular attention to environmental protection (i.e., forestry projects increased with significant conservation and environmental protection aspects); (ii) water resources management, research, and extension requirements including integrated pest management and farming systems approaches; (iii) more attention to policy dialogue based on stronger sector work; (iv) increased attention to trade issues; (v) greater involvement of nongovernment organizations (NGOs) to

[27]   ADB. 1993. *The Strategic Context of Bank Involvement in the Telecommunications Sector.* Manila.
[28]   ADB. 1992. *Operational Agenda for the GCI IV Period (1994–1998).* Manila.

Box 6: Synthesis of Postevaluation Findings in the Irrigation and Rural Development Sector

Operations of the Asian Development Bank in irrigation and rural development constituted one of the primary areas of Bank intervention and were generally directed toward surface and groundwater development and expansion and upgrading of rural infrastructure including health, water supply, and road facilities. The overall performance of projects in the irrigation and rural development sector was poor. Less than half (40.4%) of postevaluated projects were rated *generally successful*, 47.4% were rated *partly successful*, and about 12.2% were regarded as *unsuccessful*. The Bank's experience highlighted the complex character of irrigation and rural development projects, and the difficulties associated with implementing such projects. Although Bank operations in the sector have contributed to improvements in agricultural productivity and farm incomes, further scope was identified for enhancing agricultural production and alleviating rural poverty.

- **Preparation and design.** A major factor that affected project performance was inadequate preparation and design. The lack of feasibility studies or poor feasibility study preparation combined with inadequate consideration of the socioeconomic, institutional, sociocultural, topographical, geographical, and hydrological conditions in the project areas, and noninvolvement of beneficiaries in project selection contributed to less than satisfactory outcomes.

- **Policy environment.** The success of irrigation and rural development projects was found to depend critically on the efficiency and effectiveness of the policy base governing the agricultural sector. To guide policy reforms and facilitate implementation of appropriate pricing policies and structural changes, policy covenants should be time-bound, specific, monitorable, and action-oriented. The Bank, on its part, should have continuing dialogues with the governments to ensure that policy-based reforms are clearly understood and appropriately implemented.

- **Stakeholder participation.** The involvement of beneficiaries in the design, implementation, and management of small and medium-scale projects fostered a sense of ownership and cooperation among them and promoted self-reliance and less dependence on already constrained government resources. With greater beneficiary involvement in the day-to-day operations and maintenance of irrigation systems, cost recovery could be improved.

- **Monitoring and evaluation.** For benefit monitoring and evaluation to be effective, the inherent constraints to implementing such systems, such as lack of understanding of the conceptual parameters, inadequate logistical support, poor staff capabilities, and complexity of the system designs, should be addressed during project formulation and appropriate remedial measures should be built into the framework of project designs.

- **Water resource management.** Competing demands for water arising from urbanization and industrialization of developing member countries called for a total water resources management approach during project design. This would help identify priorities in relation to the varied needs for irrigation, domestic use, energy generation, and other industrial uses.

- **Project supervision.** Lessons from experience also confirmed the need for increased Bank supervision. The diversity of Bank operations in irrigation and rural development projects required more frequent visits to project sites, a multidisciplinary approach to project or program supervision, and an increased skill mix in the composition of Bank missions.

Source: ADB. 1995. *Sector Synthesis of Postevaluation Findings in the Irrigation and Rural Development Sector*. Manila.

support local community participation; (vi) greater emphasis on rural development; and (vii) stronger loan administration and project supervision.

In line with these new priorities, agriculture projects increasingly included components directly aimed at reducing poverty, enhancing the role of women, and protecting the environment.

The Bank's first agricultural project exclusively targeting women as beneficiaries was approved in 1990 for Bangladesh.[29] Likewise, the Upper Sagarmatha Agricultural Development Project in Nepal aimed to provide nonformal education and skills to women in Nepal.[30] In Sri Lanka, the Bank's Southern Province Rural Development Project taught computer skills to women to widen their

[29] ADB. 1990. *Report and Recommendation of the President to the Board of Directors: Proposed Loan and TA Grants—Rural Women Employment Creation*. Manila (Loan 1067).

[30] ADB. 1991. *Report and Recommendation of the President to the Board of Directors: Proposed Loan and TA Grants—Upper Samantha Agricultural Development*. Manila (Loan 1114).

employment opportunities.[31] In 1988, the Bank's first direct support for NGOs was introduced through the NGO-Microcredit Project[32] and the Sorsogon Integrated Area Development Project in the Philippines.[33] These projects addressed the needs of the rural poor through the provision of extremely small credits channeled through NGOs. Both aimed at alleviating poverty through job creation, with women targeted as major beneficiaries. Program lending remained an important feature facilitating policy reforms, institutional strengthening, and investment in high-priority programs, while alleviating foreign exchange problems. Private sector initiatives were also encouraged in most projects.

A new Bank policy for the forestry sector was approved in 1995 emphasizing three key principles: protection, production, and participation.[34] Under the policy, a new framework for coordinated action for forestry development in DMCs was introduced, linking both ecological and economic concerns. Several priority areas were identified, including the improvement of DMCs' policy and regulatory frameworks for forestry development; support for technological, policy and valuation research, public consultations in forestry development, development of investment strategies, and raising the capability of forestry agencies for sector analysis, planning, regulation, enforcement, and monitoring.

A new policy paper on agriculture and natural resources research (also approved in 1995) identified new challenges.[35] Despite impressive accomplishments in agricultural research, poverty and population pressures persisted while land and water resources were becoming increasingly scarce and degraded. Against this background, the new policy recommended that ADB support focus on (i) developing sustainable and remunerative

farming systems for poor farmers, (ii) ensuring sustainable management of agriculture and natural resources, and (iii) raising agricultural productivity. Under the policy, ADB committed to provide at least $5 million a year to the Consultative Group on International Agricultural Research centers and to strengthen its assistance to other national research centers.

4. Finance

ADB support to the finance sector reached $4.7 billion over 1987–1996 (compared to $1.7 billion in the previous decade) accounting for 11% of total ADB lending. The bulk of this assistance (80%) was financed from OCR. In the past, ADB assistance to the finance sector remained primarily focused on development finance institutions (DFIs). In 1987, ADB reviewed its policies on credit lines to DFIs, and concluded that the Bank's use of DFIs to assist the orderly development of DMC private sector industry had been effective and should continue.[36] However, the focus of ADB's financial sector operations should be redirected to the broader objective of developing efficient and modern financial systems that can provide a diversified range of products and services. Toward this end, the use of various modalities of assistance such as policy advice, TA, program lending, credit lines to intermediaries, and equity investments was to be encouraged. ADB should support reforms to enlarge private ownership in the sector, enhance the autonomy of state-owned intermediaries, and improve their efficiency and asset quality. Moreover, ADB should contribute to the development of capital markets by helping intermediaries develop their capacity to undertake investment financing, and by supporting the growth, diversification, and modernization of securities markets. ADB should also support

[31] ADB. 1991. *Report and Recommendation of the President to the Board of Directors: Proposed Loan and TA Grants—Southern Province Rural Development Project.* Manila (Loan 1128).
[32] ADB. 1988. *Report and Recommendation of the President to the Board of Directors: Proposed Loan—NGO-Microcredit—and TA Grants for the Microenterprise Sector and for the Strengthening of NGOs (Philippines).* Manila (Loan 940).
[33] ADB. 1988. *Report and Recommendation of the President to the Board of Directors: Proposed Loan—Sorsogon Integrated Area Development and TA Grant—Community Mobilization and Development (Philippines).* Manila (Loan 915).
[34] ADB. 1995. *The Bank's Policy on Forestry.* Manila.
[35] ADB. 1995. *The Bank's Policy on Agriculture and Natural Resources Research.* Manila.
[36] ADB. 1987. *Review of Bank Policies on Credit Lines to Development Finance Institutions.* Manila.

measures to ensure the stability and orderly growth of DMC financial services industries under effective prudential regulation and supervision.[36]

Consequently and in line with these policy directions, ADB financial sector operations broadened, with less than half (48%) of total lending supporting banking systems subsector (compared to 75% in the previous decade). Finance sector development and money and capital markets were new areas of focus, accounting for 21% and 10% of total lending in this sector, respectively. The rest went to small and medium enterprise finance and leasing (9%), investment funds (8%), microfinance (2%), housing finance (1%), and insurance and contractual savings (0.4%). Bank operations were tailored according to the specific needs of individual DMCs. For instance, assistance to transition economies included projects that transferred banking skills or supported the upgrading of banking regulation and supervision. In South Asian economies where financial sectors were dominated by public banks, attention was placed on deregulation, while improving prudential and regulatory mechanisms. Meanwhile, in more advanced financial markets, ADB worked with DMCs to develop their capital markets to facilitate long-term domestic debt financing to meet the region's rapidly growing infrastructure requirements.[37]

5.   Social Sectors[38]

In recognition of the importance of better social services to enhance the quality of people's life and promote growth in the longer term, social sector lending increased.[39]

Water Supply and Sanitation and Urban Development. Total ADB lending for water supply and other municipal infrastructure projects reached $3.6 billion from 1987 to 1996, compared to $1.6 billion in the second decade. The sector's

share in total lending decreased slightly from 10% to 8% over the same period. Around three-fourths of sector lending was funded from OCR. The top country recipients were: Indonesia (33%), the PRC (16%), the Philippines (14%), Pakistan (7%), and Bangladesh (6%). The main objective of the Bank's involvement in the sector was to improve health and living standards, thereby contributing to poverty reduction and environmental improvement. Urban sector development was given increased attention, accounting for 53% of total lending in this sector (compared to 22% in the previous decade). The remaining share of lending went to water supply and sanitation (38%), and waste management (8%). Bank-financed rural water supply projects sought to promote and strengthen community participation. Cost recovery and sustainability were emphasized and appropriate incentives structures were sought to adequately reflect economic costs. Water conservation through demand management and effective tariff policies was also encouraged.

ADB had been providing assistance for urban development and housing as a separate subsector since 1976. ADB reviewed its operations in the subsector in 1987.[40] The review concluded that physical infrastructure such as improvements in slum and squatter settlements, low-income housing and water supply, and sanitation should continue to receive Bank assistance. In addition, problems created by rural–urban migration, rapid urbanization, and the explosive growth of megacities should receive increased attention. To this end and given that the institutional structure and policies for urban development in most DMCs were usually not well articulated, sector studies, institutional strengthening, and policy dialogue for rationalization of pricing, revenue generation, and urban development financing would require additional support. ADB should also do more to integrate private sector activities in urban projects.

---

[37]   See also ADB. 1987. *Review of the Bank's Recent Initiatives for Assistance in the Development of Capital Markets in DMCs.* Manila; ADB. 1991. Bank Assistance to Development Finance Institutions. Memo to the Board. Manila.

[38]   At the time, social sectors referred to education, health and population, urban development and housing, and water supply and sanitation.

[39]   This was in line with the recommendations of a report on the Bank's Role in the 1990s. See ADB.1989. *Asian Development Bank in 1990s: Report of a Panel.* Manila.

[40]   ADB. 1987. *Review of the Bank Operations in the Urban Development and Housing Sector.* Manila.

Education. A review of the Bank's role in the education sector was carried out in 1987–1988, resulting in a new approach, *Education and Development in Asia and Pacific*, endorsed by the Board in March 1989.[41] The new policy widened ADB's operational scope from a narrow focus on technical and vocational education and training to an approach that embraced the entire sector. Consequently, total education lending jumped from $806 million over 1977–1986 to $2.3 billion in the succeeding 10 years, accounting for 5% of total lending (same as in the previous decade). ADB operations now covered virtually the entire sector, including primary education and nonformal education. In 1989, the first ADB loan to primary education was approved, which was also the first loan focused on girls.[42] Support to technical and vocational education and training continued, which accounted for the largest share of sector lending (32% down from 49% in the previous decade). At the same time, greater emphasis was placed on preprimary and basic education (now accounting for 30% of total sector lending compared to 5% in the previous decade). Support to tertiary and higher education accounted for 21% of sector lending, with support aimed at making higher education more responsive to the needs of emerging market economies. Over time, the focus also shifted from physical facilities to a greater proportion of "software" (i.e., curriculum and institutional development and sectoral planning and management). Structural reforms of upper secondary education were promoted, representing 10% of total lending for this sector. The rest went to education sector development (4%) and nonformal education including distance education methods (3%). Education sector lending was primarily financed (56%) from OCR. The top country recipients were Indonesia (49%), Pakistan (13%), Bangladesh (12%), Malaysia (6%), and the Philippines (5%).

Health, Social Protection, and Population. Health sector lending jumped from $329 million over 1977–1986 to $904 million in the succeeding 10 years, accounting for 2% of total lending (same as in the previous decade). ADB's main objective in the sector was to improve equity, accessibility, quality, and efficiency at the primary health care level and to ensure efficient functioning of health referral networks. The involvement of NGOs was encouraged in the process. Besides expanding and improving infrastructure, the management and financing of health systems was strengthened, and assistance for control of communicable disease also increased significantly. Overall, 40% of total lending to this sector went to health systems, 33% to social protection (a new area), 22% to health programs, and 5% to nutrition. Around three-fourths of lending for the health sector was funded from ADF. The top borrowers were Pakistan (46%), Indonesia (14%), Malaysia (12%), the Philippines (9%), and Bangladesh (6%).

In many DMCs, rapid population growth eroded the gains from economic growth and made it more difficult to reduce poverty. Yet, the Bank's role in population activities had not been significant and was limited mostly to small population components in integrated health and population projects. In 1992, ADB's commitment in this area was strengthened when population planning was identified as a medium-term strategic objective in the MTSF, 1992–1995. The MTSF called for an expansion of ADB's assistance for population planning activities, including (i) continued integration of health and population activities (but including the possibility of stand-alone population projects); (ii) improved accessibility of family planning services; (iii) institutional strengthening of family planning programs; and (iv) inclusion of population-related activities in projects in other

---

[41] ADB. 1991. *Education and Development in Asia and the Pacific*. Manila.

[42] ADB approved its first loan to primary education in 1989 in Pakistan (Loan 977-PAK); general secondary education in 1988 in the Philippines (Loan 898-PHI) and nonformal education in rural training in 1990 in Bangladesh (Loan 1066-BAN). Primary and nonformal education was given increased attention, as parts of efforts to target women and underserved populations.

sectors. In 1993, the Bank approved its first stand-alone population project in Papua New Guinea.[43] In 1994, ADB approved a new policy on population.[44] The policy endorsed a three-pronged approach for the Bank. First, assistance would be provided to reduce gender disparities in school enrolment, since educated women were the most persistent advocates of small families. Second, attention would be paid to safeguarding women's reproductive health, since safe pregnancy and childbirth were seen as precursors to fertility decline. Third, ADB efforts would seek to make access to family services more equitable.

D. Cross-Cutting and Thematic Issues

1. Growth and Policy Reform

The Bank's traditional approach to fostering economic growth in its DMCs was through the financing of development projects. However, the economic difficulties experienced by some DMCs in the 1980s and the deterioration of the global economic environment for development meant that restoring DMCs (especially the poorest ones) to a sustained growth path required increasing emphasis on macroeconomic stabilization and policy reform. The lead in these efforts was taken by the Bretton Woods institutions. Over the decade, the Bank increasingly sought to play its part through policy dialogue primarily at the sector level. The Bank's policy agenda encompassed a wide range of issues, including the regulatory and legal framework for growth, trade and investment regimes, relative role of the private and public sectors, pricing and tariffs, cost recovery, good governance, decentralization, beneficiary participation, and social and environmental issues. ADB's greater emphasis on policy reforms led to an increased use of TA and adjustment to its program lending instrument to give it a stronger policy focus (see section V.A).

2. Poverty

While a number of ADB projects had benefited the poor, it was felt that a more systematic and focused approach was needed, given the magnitude of the poverty problem in the region. An internal Task Force on Poverty Alleviation was established in 1988 and suggested a dual approach to the problem.[45] On one hand, the Bank should pay more attention to poverty issues during the formulation and implementation of traditional projects. This meant that ADB should identify target groups among the poor more clearly, involve beneficiaries in project development and implementation, decentralize decision-making as much as possible, and undertake socioeconomic analyses as the basis for specifying, monitoring, and guiding projects activities. On the other hand, the Bank should supplement this approach with projects specifically designed to alleviate poverty. These included projects on social infrastructure and environment, projects designed to increase income and employment opportunities and increase access to basic social services, and sector development and/or adjustment programs to support DMCs' poverty alleviation efforts (specifically in the education and health sectors). In addition, the Bank should intensify its economic and sector work related to poverty (Box 7).

Over the decade, ADB's lending was consciously reoriented to balance economic growth objectives with social objectives. ADB established a medium-term target of achieving a 50/50 lending mix between traditional activities (i.e., growth-oriented projects) and newer efforts like poverty reduction, human resource development, and environmental protection. In parallel, ADB adjusted its approach within key sectors. Poverty issues were also considered systematically during country strategy and operational programming exercises (Table 2).

---

[43] ADB. 1993. *Report and Recommendation of the President to the Board of Directors: Proposed Loan to Papua New Guinea for the Population and Planning Project*. Manila (Loan 1225).

[44] ADB. 1994. *Population Policy Paper: Framework for Bank Assistance to the Population Sector*. Manila (R80-94).

[45] ADB. 1988. *Task Force Report on the Bank's Role in Poverty Alleviation*. Manila.

Box 7: Poverty in Asia

Throughout the decade, the Asian Development Bank (ADB) intensified its research and analytical work relating to poverty reduction. Two major research projects on rural and urban poverty were undertaken in selected developing member countries (DMCs), financed through regional technical assistance. A number of publications emerged from these studies including a book entitled *Rural Poverty in Asia: Priority Issues and Policy Options* copublished by Oxford University Press.

These studies confirmed that the poverty problem in Asia was largely a rural phenomenon. In terms of incidence, about a third to a half of the rural population was considered poor in Bangladesh, India, Pakistan, the Philippines, and Sri Lanka. Compounding the problem of rural poverty was the rising incidence of urban poverty caused by accelerating urbanization and urban population growth in DMCs. In Indonesia and the Republic of Korea, the incidence of poverty was higher in urban than in rural areas. With rapid urbanization expected to continue in the future, urban poverty was expected to be a persistent problem in DMCs, one that may diminish more slowly than rural poverty.

The DMCs were making significant efforts to reduce poverty, with some making greater headway than others. The single most important factor underlying the success of DMCs in poverty reduction was economic growth. Thus in the newly industrializing economies (NIEs), such as the Republic of Korea and Taipei,China and in quasi-NIEs, such as Indonesia, Malaysia, and Thailand, total poverty incidence was cut to half or even less in 10–15 years. In the Republic of Korea, poverty incidence was reported to be below 5%, while in Indonesia, Malaysia, and Thailand, it ranged from 15% to 20%. There was also dramatic progress in the People's Republic of China. In countries with relatively poor to modest economic performance, such as South Asian DMCs and the Philippines, poverty reduction was correspondingly slow and somewhat less clear. Poverty incidence in these countries remained at 30%–45%, and in some cases, the actual number of poor people appeared to be on the rise. Given the strategic role of economic growth in poverty reduction, sound macroeconomic (fiscal, monetary, exchange rate, and trade) and sectoral (agricultural and industrial) policies to promote growth were deemed critically important. In many DMCs until the late 1980s, the economic policy framework was unfavorable. However, in the early 1990s, most DMCs embarked on major policy reforms aimed at liberalizing their economy, expanding opportunities for the private sector, and increasing global competitiveness.

The emerging policy environment in these DMCs was thus expected to be more conducive to economic growth and poverty reduction.

Sources: ADB. 1994. ADF VI: Progress Report. Manila; M. G. Quibria, ed. 1994. *Rural Poverty in Asia: Priority Issues and Policy Options*. Manila: Asian Development Bank.

Table 2: Classification of Projects by Objective, 1993–1996

Classification	1993 Number	%	1994 Number	%	1995 Number	%	1996 Number	%	1993–1996 Number	%
Traditional Growth Projects[a]	28	45	24	51	25	38	30	39	107	43
Social Projects	22	35	10	21	21	32	31	41	84	34
Poverty Reduction	4	6	0	0	4	6	9	12	17	7
Human Development	17	27	9	19	17	26	21	28	64	26
Women in Development	1	2	1	2	0	0	1	1	3	1
Environmental Projects	2	4	1	2	5	8	8	11	16	6
Growth-Oriented Projects[b]	10	16	12	26	14	22	7	9	43	17
Total	62	100	47	100	65	100	76	100	250	100

a   A project was classified as a growth project if its primary aim is to promote economic growth through investments that increase economic production capacity and/or enhance economic efficiency.

b   A project was classified as a growth-oriented project if social emphasis is a secondary aim.

Notes: Loan projects were classified based on a new project classification system introduced in 1992. The number of loan projects excludes private sector loans and/or equity, and technical assistance loans.

Source: ADB. 1997. *Annual Report 1996*. Manila. p.88.

The Bank also strengthened in-house capacity and techniques for undertaking poverty operations. In 1991, the *Guidelines for the Social Analysis of Development Projects* were issued to ensure that social aspects of a project's design were taken into account on a uniform basis.[46] A Social Dimensions Unit was established in 1992 to integrate cross-cutting social dimensions, including poverty reduction, women in development, human resource development, and the avoidance or mitigation of any adverse effects of development interventions on vulnerable groups. The major goal of this unit was to help staff and DMCs incorporate these dimensions into their operations.

The importance given to poverty projects also led ADB to intensify its cooperation with NGOs, especially those that operate at the local level. ADB had earlier established a framework to promote greater and more effective cooperation with NGOs in 1987.[47] The policy highlighted how the Bank could enhance the effectiveness of its operations by drawing upon NGOs in certain niche areas where there was strong potential for expansion and cooperation (i.e., rural development, small-scale industry, social infrastructure, and environmental protection). Over the decade, the bulk of the Bank's cooperation was concentrated in those sectors, particularly in projects aimed at poverty reduction and environmental protection and management. In these projects, ADB sought to "put people first," which necessitated assessment of people's needs, demands, and absorptive capacity, as well as their active participation in the project cycle. To this end, ADB found it useful to involve NGOs in all stages of the project cycle. This form of cooperation grew over the decade. TA was also provided to NGOs to improve their project preparation and implementation capabilities (e.g., enhancing the managerial capacities of NGOs participating in Bank-financed microcredit projects in the Philippines).[48] On a selective basis, the Bank also helped NGOs to organize seminars on issues of mutual interest.[49]

In 1995, ADB approved a new policy on involuntary resettlement to ensure that people displaced by Bank projects receive assistance (preferably under the project), so that they would be at least as well off as they would have been in the absence of the project.[50] Consideration of vulnerable groups was also regarded as an important means to improve project quality and project implementation, especially in cases where land had to be acquired and persons resettled.[51] Substantial work was completed on a policy to address indigenous peoples. Participatory approaches were considered as important elements to allow individuals and groups to identify, formulate, implement, and evaluate policies, programs, and policies that affect them. It was also considered to be a powerful means of enhancing ownership and support for Bank activities. A handbook was published in 1996 on mainstreaming participatory development processes in operations that described how ADB aimed to institutionalize participatory development processes in all stages of the project cycle.[52]

3.   Women in Development

The issue of women in development (WID) continued to receive increasing attention. In 1985, the Bank adopted a policy on WID whose main thrust was integration of gender consideration into all aspects of operations, i.e., addressing the role of women and the effects of projects on them, at every stage of the project cycle. Emphasis was given to projects in the social

---

[46]   ADB. 1993. *Guidelines for Incorporation of Social Dimensions in Bank Operations*. Manila; ADB. 1994. *A Handbook for the Incorporation of Social Dimensions Projects*. Manila.

[47]   ADB. 1987. *The Bank's Cooperation with Non-governmental Organizations*. Manila (R79-87).

[48]   ADB. 1988. *Technical Assistance to the Philippines for Institutional Strengthening of NGOs*. Manila (TA 1093-PHI); ADB. 1992. *Technical Assistance to the Philippines for NGO Development Program and Institutional Strengthening of DTI*. Manila (TA 1842-PHI).

[49]   ADB. 1992. *Technical Assistance for Regional Workshop on Banking with the Poor*. Manila (TA 5496).

[50]   ADB. 1995. *Involuntary Resettlement*. Manila.

[51]   ADB. 1996. *Handbook on Resettlement: A Guide to Good Practice*. Manila.

[52]   ADB. 1996. *Mainstreaming Participatory Development Processes into Bank Operations*. Manila.

sectors that provide direct benefits to women and in sectors such as agriculture, rural development, and small-scale industries that provide employment opportunities for women. Financing of stand-alone, women-targeted projects was also given priority. As a basis for the Bank's work in this area, WID country briefing papers were prepared for most DMCs.[53] At the same time, gender-disaggregated data were prepared and collected to monitor changes in the status and participation of women in each DMC.

The Social Dimension Unit was in charge of coordinating and monitoring WID activities and for sharpening their focus. There was also a shift over the decade, from an emphasis on project-specific activities to "mainstreaming." The revised operational framework stressed (i) promotion of women-friendly macro policies; (ii) gender analysis in all projects; (iii) equal access of women to project inputs, including participatory aspects; (iv) project components exclusively targeted for generating employment for women; and (v) social service projects with preferable access for women. Since country operational strategy studies set the stage for future Bank activities in a DMC, WID concerns were to be integrated at the country level (in these studies) to ensure that the specific needs and concerns of women in that country were adequately addressed.

4.   Environment

Environmental lending increased considerably, from 4% of total lending in 1991 to 11% in 1996). ADB's efforts centered on three areas: (i) comprehensive environmental assessment of all Bank-financed projects, (ii) financing of projects that address environmental concerns, and (iii) strengthening the capacity of borrowers for environmental assessment and other aspects of environmental planning and management. The preparatory efforts for ADB's participation at the Earth Summit in Rio de Janeiro in 1992 (where President Tarumizu led the ADB

delegation); the subsequent identification of actions to respond to Agenda 21; and the dialogue with DMCs on ways of meeting the monitoring and reporting requirements of the United Nations Conference on Environment and Development, helped give greater impetus to these initiatives. ADB's Environment Unit, which was created in 1987, was upgraded into a division in 1989, and further converted to the Office of the Environment in 1990.

ADB systematically screened all proposed projects for their expected environmental impact. In 1992, the criteria employed for this purpose were modified to align with the system followed by the World Bank and other international financial institutions. To ensure consistency in coverage and quality, the format of environmental impact assessments was standardized. In addition, environment sector reports were prepared for each DMC and regularly updated as an input to country strategy and country programming work. Environmental considerations were also integrated in sector operations. For example, industry sector lending included large investment for energy conservation and environmental improvement in several DMCs. In terms of institution building, ADB assisted DMCs to enhance their level of environmental management to formulate policies, strategies, and legislation; and strengthen mechanisms for participation of NGOs. Capacity building also covered staff capability for undertaking environmental impact assessments. Direct environmental lending supported (i) pollution control; (ii) energy conservation and end-use efficiency; (iii) marine, water, land, and soil resource management and conservation; (iv) environment improvement in both rural and urban areas; (v) interlinked poverty and environmental improvement; and (vi) tropical forest management and conservation of biological diversity. In addition, the Bank encouraged regional and global cooperation on environmental issues.

---

[53] A country briefing paper is prepared as a background document to ADB's country operational strategy to ensure mainstreaming of gender considerations. Through these papers, the Bank began to incorporate consideration of gender issues into the programming activities of each DMC. In 1986, WID briefing papers were prepared for Bangladesh, Indonesia, and Thailand.

5. Private Sector

Bank assistance to the private sector started with credit lines to DFIs. In 1983, ADB took a major initiative in directly assisting the private sector in its DMCs by introducing an equity investment facility. Support to the private sector was further strengthened in 1985 with the approval of lending to the private sector without government guarantees. The Board paper envisaged a review of the policy after 2 years. An interim study of the Bank's private sector operations was completed in 1987.[54] A comprehensive review was submitted to the Board in 1988.[55] Some changes were made to allow more responsiveness to private sector needs and to enable the Bank to play a more catalytic role. As a result of the review, amounts allocated for loans without government guarantees were raised from $145 million to $375 million. Greater flexibility was introduced with respect to the size of equity investments and loans. The commitment fee for loan to private sector companies was also reduced.

In 1989, a Private Sector Department was created to act as the focal point for private sector activities within the Bank. ADB also invested $35 million in the Asian Finance and Investment Corporation (AFIC) to complement ADB's direct private sector operations. This was seen as part of a series of initiatives to strengthen ADB's developmental role in strengthening and diversifying the institutional structure for financing private enterprises in its DMCs. ADB's association and seed money enabled AFIC to mobilize substantial additional funds by way of equity and borrowings from other sources for channeling into productive private enterprises in DMCs. ADB would be AFIC's largest, though minority, shareholder, with the remaining equity being held by leading financial institutions of diverse specialization both within and outside the region.[56]

Given the rapid development of the Bank's private sector activities, another review was undertaken in 1990.[57] The review highlighted the need for a flexible response to the requirement of private enterprises depending on the economic environment, government policies, and availability of project finance resources in each DMC. The review concluded that, as an agent of change, ADB should focus on operations that have qualities of demonstrability, catalytic function, and policy dialogue. Increasing private sector operations could require administrative and procedural changes over time. A more comprehensive review of private sector operations (including DFI lending) was therefore needed to identify possible ramifications of such changes. The Board also approved an increase in the existing ceiling of $375 million for private sector investments without government guarantees to $1 billion.

In March 1991, a private sector task force established to explore institutional and human resource requirements for effective private sector operations expressed concern that ADB's private sector activities lacked an overall, unifying operational framework, and tended to be selected on an ad hoc basis. It therefore recommended that ADB bring them more in tandem with its public sector program.[58] In response, private sector operations were integrated into the Bank's overall operational activities in 1992. A Private Sector Support Unit was created to (i) advise on privatization, financing of projects through build–operate–transfer or build–operate–own schemes, and capital markets; (ii) assist operational departments in promoting and facilitating private sector alternatives and project formulation; (iii) undertake regional operations in capital markets and financial sector development; and (iv) assume responsibilities for portfolio management. In addition, staff of the Private Sector Department were redeployed to resident missions to help evaluate and process private sector projects.

A *Strategy for the Bank's Assistance for Private Sector Development* was approved in 1995.[59] It sharpened

---

[54] ADB. 1987. *An Interim Review of Bank Policy and Procedures for Private Sector Operations.* Manila.
[55] ADB. 1988. *A Review of Private Sector Operations.* Manila.
[56] Following the market difficulties AFIC faced during the Asian financial crisis, ADB decided to eventually cease its support for AFIC.
[57] ADB. 1990. *Second Review of Private Sector Operations.* Manila.
[58] ADB. 1992. *Report of the Private Sector Task Force.* Manila.
[59] ADB. 1995. *Strategy for the Bank's Assistance for Private Sector Development.* Manila.

the focus of the Bank's private sector operations and reconfirmed the importance of TA support and policy advice to improve the environment for private sector development, particularly in terms of policy, legal and regulatory reforms, institutional enhancements, and human development. The formulation and implementation of reforms should continue to be supported, on a selective basis, through program lending. In terms of direct financing of private sector projects, priority should be given to capital markets and infrastructure development. The strategy also recommended that private sector development be dovetailed with country operational strategy studies and country assistance programs to increase the synergy between public and private sector operations.

6. Regional Cooperation

Support for regional cooperation is a fundamental part of ADB's operations. The ADB Charter gives it a mandate to foster economic cooperation in the region. The nature of the Bank's involvement in this area evolved over the years, in line with the needs of its DMCs. In its early years, ADB coordinated studies for a number of subregional projects. ADB also contributed to regional research institutions, such as the International Rice Research Institute and the Asian Productivity Organization; and sponsored major regional surveys such as the Asian Agriculture Survey (1967 and 1976), the Asian Industrial Survey (1971), the Southeast Asian Regional Transport Survey (1968), and the Regional Energy Survey (1980). Over the third decade, ADB's support gained momentum and became more diversified. It grew from an average of $700,000 a year in the 1970s to around $17.5 million a year in the second half of the decade (1991–1996).

ADB's first MTSF (1992–1995) signaled an expanded role for the Bank in promoting regional cooperation as one of its strategic objectives. It identified three complementary functions for the Bank in this area. First, through its research and TA activities, ADB could provide information to increase DMCs' understanding of the importance and benefits of cooperation in areas such as trade, investment, finance, technology, infrastructure, natural and human resource development, and environmental protection. Second, because of its nonpartisan character, the Bank was in a position to act as an "honest broker," playing an important supportive role by encouraging dialogue, suggesting approaches, and identifying possible projects. Third, as a development catalyst, the Bank could provide its own funds to support regional cooperation but also help mobilize funds from other sources.

The Bank supported regional cooperation in the Greater Mekong Subregion (GMS). It funded a comprehensive study of the prospects for such cooperation among the six GMS countries, namely, Cambodia, the Lao PDR, Myanmar, Thailand, Viet Nam, and Yunnan Province in the PRC. A series of reports was prepared to identify the scope, opportunities, benefits, costs, and mechanisms for enhancing cooperation. The transport and energy sectors were identified as essential to expanding subregional cooperation and detailed sector studies were prepared. Many possible actions were also identified in the areas of tourism, trade, investment, environment, and human resource development. The GMS Program was officially launched in 1992 and would become one of ADB's largest and most successful regional programs (Box 8).

ADB also actively promoted the concept of growth triangles. In early 1993, at the request of the governments concerned, it initiated a study on the Indonesia–Malaysia–Thailand growth triangle. A similar study done in 1994–1995 explored the potential for an east ASEAN growth area involving Brunei Darussalam, Indonesia, Malaysia, and the Philippines. Both studies concluded that complementarities across countries were strong enough for substantial cooperation. ADB also supported studies on specific regional issues (capital market development, population control, environmental protection, etc.). Annual forums such as development roundtables, workshops on Asian economic outlook, and conferences on development economics provided occasions for policy dialogue on matters concerning the region as a whole.

> ## Box 8: An Enduring Commitment to the Greater Mekong Subregion
>
> In his address at the 1972 Annual Meeting of the Asian Development Bank (ADB), President Takeshi Watanabe said: "Our least developed members hold special claim on our attention... that commitment has extended to the war-torn countries of the Mekong Basin, where loans and technical assistance have been forthcoming to Cambodia, the Lao People's Democratic Republic (Lao PDR), and the Socialist Republic of Viet Nam." He added, "Development is not easy amid the destruction of war... but we have not avoided our responsibility to bring development to the people of that region."
>
> ADB's second President, Shiro Inoue, also believed that ADB, as an Asian institution, should play an important role in the economic reconstruction of Southeast Asia and made this one of his special priorities. Under his leadership, the Bank joined the World Bank in convening a meeting of potential donors in 1975 in the Lao PDR, to help the reconstruction of Southeast Asia. But peace and development remained elusive, and the subregion continued to be plagued by conflict, massive destruction, and historic divisions among neighboring countries.
>
> It was not until 1992 that the Greater Mekong Subregion (GMS) Economic Cooperation Program would be formally established. It covered six countries: Cambodia, the Lao PDR, Myanmar, Thailand, Viet Nam, and Yunnan province in the People's Republic of China. ADB assumed the role of Secretariat as well as facilitator, financier, honest broker, and technical adviser. The uncertainties surrounding the relationships among the various countries required flexibility in the design and selection of priority projects for cooperation. During its initial years, the program focused on establishing a platform for GMS policymakers to meet, discuss, and explore avenues for cooperation. These early initiatives (financed primarily through regional technical assistance) contributed to building mutual trust and goodwill among the countries. ADB's approach was pragmatic. For ADB and the early architects of the GMS, the first step in linking together disparate countries was the simple act of building roads, bridges, and other infrastructure investments that would provide clear benefits to at least two participating countries. In 1994, ADB brokered two such projects, the Yunnan Expressway (in the PRC) and Theun Hinboun Hydropower Project (in the Lao PDR).
>
> This gradual approach eventually paid off as the GMS countries became more confident in their relationships. ADB's independent evaluation concluded that ADB's pragmatic and activity-based approach (compared with the rules-based approach of other regional cooperation schemes) proved to be effective in generating early and tangible results. This approach would become a template for other subregional economic cooperation activities, and was adopted in ADB's first regional cooperation strategy.
>
> Since then, the GMS has witnessed a dramatic transformation. The GMS Program would deepen in the next decade, as the 1997 Asian financial crisis would further strengthen the countries' resolve to pursue regional cooperation, eventually leading to a 10-year GMS Strategic Framework (2002–2012) forged during the first GMS Leaders' Summit in 2002. This would mark an important turning point for the GMS Program as countries, previously torn by war and conflict, came together to cement their commitment to a shared vision of an integrated, prosperous, and harmonious subregion.
>
> Sources: ADB. 2004. *Bank Support for Regional Cooperation*. Manila (R60-94); ADB. 2000. *The Greater Mekong Subregional Economic Cooperation Program Assistance Plan: 2001–2003*. Manila; ADB. 1999. *Impact Evaluation Study of the ADB's Subregional Economic Cooperation Program in the Greater Mekong Subregion*. Manila; ADB. 1994. *Report of the Recommendation of the President to the Board of Directors: Proposed Loan and Technical Assistance Grants–Heilongjiang and Yunnan Expressways Projects (People's Republic of China)*. Manila (Loan 1325); ADB. 1994. *Report of the Recommendation of the President to the Board of Directors: Proposed Loan–Theun-Hinboun Hydropower Project (Lao People's Democratic Republic)*. Manila (Loan 1329).

In 1994, ADB adopted a regional cooperation policy.[60] The policy proposed a three-phased approach to guide ADB's initial regional cooperation activities. In the first phase, ADB was expected to raise awareness of DMCs on the importance of regional cooperation through information dissemination, with the overall aim of building mutual respect, confidence, and trust among DMCs. In the second phase, potential regional projects and programs that could yield quick and tangible results were to be identified. In the third phase, ADB was to finance cross-border projects and national projects with a significant cross-border or regional dimension. Greater support was envisaged in areas such as intraregional trade, cooperation in technology

---

60   ADB. 1994. *Bank Support for Regional Cooperation*. Manila.

research, and management of common natural resources. Financing of loan projects (particularly in natural resource management (i.e., water and energy as well as transportation) and use of TA for regional activities (in areas such as policy support and capacity building) were to be pursued.

7.   Governance

Over the decade, there was increasing concern about governance issues in the development agenda. The issue also received attention during the fifth ADF replenishment discussions and the negotiations on ADB's fourth general capital increase (GCI IV) where the Bank was urged to address governance issues in its operations. In view of the importance and urgency of the subject, interim staff instructions on governance were issued February 1994. In 1995, ADB became the first multilateral development bank to have a Board-approved governance policy.[61] Under the new policy, governance was considered synonymous with sound development management, as it related to the effectiveness with which development assistance was used, the impact of development programs and projects (including those financed by ADB), and the absorptive capacity of borrowing DMCs.

The Bank recognized that the policy environment in which development took place should be appropriate, that equity issues should be addressed, that DMCs should strengthen their ownership of projects and take a participatory approach in project design and implementation, and that the experience of the high-performing economies in the region could be useful in formulating development strategies. To make the elements of good governance operationally relevant, four areas of focus were identified: (i) accountability (building government capacity); (ii) participation (participatory development processes); (iii) predictability (legal frameworks); and (iv) transparency (openness of information).

These dimensions were integrated into operations to raise the quality of governance in DMCs.

The Bank also sought to strengthen its internal governance and enhance its accountability to its member governments, by ensuring maximum transparency in its operations. In September 1994, the Bank approved a new policy on disclosure of information.[62] It also established procedures for its implementation and revised the classification system on the release of ADB documents. The policy encouraged a two-way flow of information and sought to promote greater local participation in decision-making and ownership of decisions, and broadened understanding of the Bank's role and support for its mission. In October 1994, the Board approved an information policy and strategy to deliver the Bank's messages more effectively in member countries.[63] The policy codified information requirements and objectives, while the strategy identified the key messages the Bank should deliver, its target audience, and the most cost-effective modes of delivery.

In December 1995, ADB approved the establishment of an inspection function to complement ADB's existing audit, supervision, and evaluation systems. The inspection function provided a forum for project beneficiaries to appeal to an independent body in relation to ADB's compliance with operational policies and procedures in its assisted projects.[64] The inspection function sought to address increased attention to accountability, transparency, and public participation by ADB and MDBs.

E.   Technical Assistance

Through its TA operations, ADB assists its DMCs in identifying, formulating, and implementing projects; improving their institutional capacities; formulating development strategies; promoting

---

[61]   ADB. 1995. *Governance: Sound Development Management*. Manila.
[62]   ADB. 1994. *Confidentiality and Disclosure of Information*. Manila.
[63]   ADB. 1994. *Information Policy and Strategy of Asian Development Bank*. Manila.
[64]   ADB. 1995. *Establishment of an Inspection Function*. Manila.

technology transfers; and fostering regional cooperation. Over the third decade, the use of TA gained prominence and became a vital element of ADB's development strategy, as the Bank sought to redefine its role from project financier to a broad based development institution, providing integrated services of financing, policy support, and capacity building. Over 1987–1996, TA operations increased dramatically, reaching $882 million (Figure 4), a sevenfold increase from the previous decade.[65] Of this amount, 82% were allocated to specific countries, while the remaining 18% funded regional TAs. The top five county recipients were the PRC (14%), Indonesia (12%), the Philippines (8%), Bangladesh (6%), and Pakistan (5%). ADB's TA operations covered a multitude of sectors and subsectors. Compared to the previous decade, there was a shift in the focal areas of assistance. Assistance in the agriculture and energy sectors decreased, accounting for 30% and 9% of TA, respectively, compared to 41% and 14% in the previous decade. In contrast, support for public sector management, transport and ICT, and

social sectors expanded (accounting for 16%, 14%, and 15%, respectively, compared to 9%, 10%, and 12% in the previous decade).

In 1988, ADB introduced various measures to streamline the processing and financing of TA. A number of TA ceilings or limits were raised, largely to reflect the increase in the remuneration of consulting services. With the expansion of TA operations, ADB was conscious of the need to ensure that these activities were not spread too wide nor too thin. Starting in 1989, the annual TA program was planned and monitored within a framework of "indicative planning figures," in terms of both numbers and amounts of TA assistance. In the case of RETA, an interdepartmental review committee was set up to examine in a comprehensive manner all aspects of the Bank's TA program. The TA program would eventually be integrated in the country programming and strategy formulation process, as well as in the Bank's multiyear planning framework. Box 9 provides an overview of the evolution of ADB's TA over the first 3 decades.

Figure 4: Technical Assistance Approvals, 1987–1996
($ million)

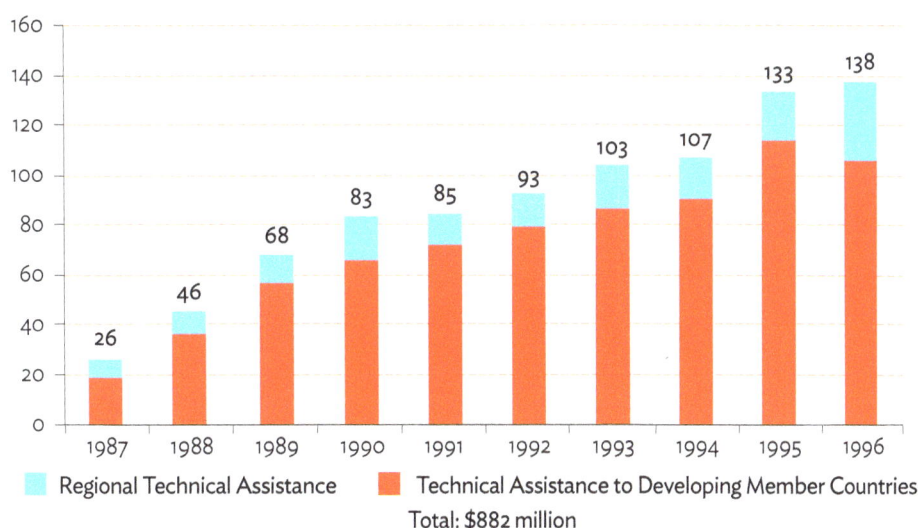

Total: $882 million

Notes: Technical assistance approvals only cover grants those funded by the Technical Assistance Special Fund and the Japan Special Fund.
Source: ADB loan, technical assistance, grant, and equity approvals database.

[65] During the first 2 decades, TA assistance represented 0.75% and 0.78% of total ADB assistance, respectively. This percentage jumped to 2% in the third decade.

Box 9: Effecting Change through Technical Assistance—Historical Perspective

Over the years, the focus of technical assistance (TA) of the Asian Development Bank (ADB) has shifted. When ADB was first established, the focus was on the preparation of projects suitable for financing. TA was used to finance feasibility studies and other project preparation work, as well as project implementation through the provision of supervision services and institutional strengthening of project executing agencies. At the time, TA was regarded primarily as a modality to support the project financing function of the Bank, which was perceived as its main function.

The emphasis changed in the second decade, as it became evident that effective development required much more than close attention to projects. More often than not, the success or failure of a project was decided not by the technical or financial quality of the project but by the economic environment, both at the macro and sector levels. The Bank responded to these findings by intensifying policy dialogue with governments in developing member countries (DMCs), introducing a policy-based lending modality (the program loan), and through increased used of TA to address key policy issues.

In the third decade, the emphasis on policy and broader institutional capacity was further intensified, and the role of TA acquired new dimensions. Many DMCs embraced market-oriented, outward-looking economic management strategies and began to undertake various policy and regulatory reforms to move in that direction. Several centrally planned economies began the process of transitioning to a market economy. At the same time, as a result of the end of the Cold War, opportunities increased for regional and subregional cooperation through enhanced trade and investment and cross-border development of infrastructure and management of natural resources. Through its TA operations, the Bank was uniquely positioned to act as a broker, promoter, and financier providing knowledge, experience, and network to support its DMCs.

Source: ADB. 1998. *Annual Report 1997.* Manila. pp. 19–39.

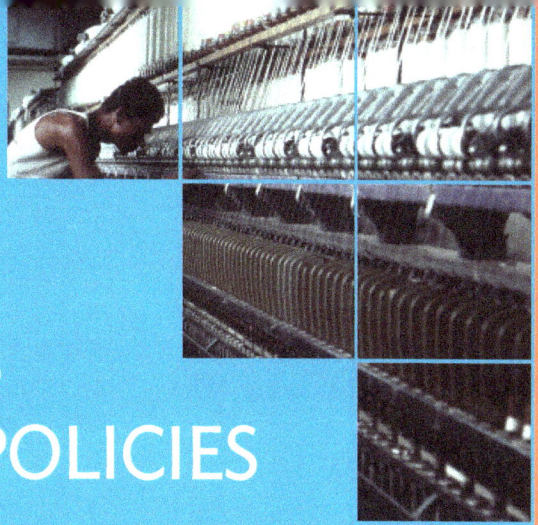

V. BUSINESS PROCESSES AND OPERATIONAL POLICIES

- In keeping with its continuing efforts to respond to evolving needs and expectations of its member countries, ADB's lending instruments and processes were adjusted and new ones were introduced.
- More emphasis was given to improving project quality, as projects grew more complex and demanding of staff efforts. A new organizational structure was introduced to ensure a strengthened country focus in operations.

A. Instruments and Modalities

1. Program Lending

Given the increased attention on policy aspects, a revised program lending instrument was introduced in 1987.[66] Since 1978, the Bank had provided program loans to promote increased capacity utilization by financing imported inputs, particularly in high-priority areas (mostly agriculture). In 1987, the objective of program loans was redefined to address underlying sector needs and constraints, including policy reforms, investment plans, and institutional strengthening. Further, the ceiling on program lending was raised from 10% to 15% of total ADB lending and the 20% ceiling for individual countries was abolished.[67] The scope of lending was broadened to include the financial, industry,

energy, transport and ICT, and social sectors. Procurement procedures were eased to facilitate faster disbursement. The new policy cautioned that program loan conditionalities should not be expected to work in the same way as for project loans; instead, they should be assessed in the broad context of policy reform. To capture this, the process should be reflected in a development policy letter from the government requesting the program loan. Reforms should be paced and transitional adjustment costs reduced by providing retraining and other adjustment assistance, especially for the poor. The policy also called for compatibility of program loans with policy reform measures of the International Monetary Fund and the World Bank. However, unlike earlier program loans, reference to a "no objection" clause from the International Monetary Fund was no longer required. In December 1987, the Bank approved

---

[66] ADB. 1987. *A Review of Program Lending Policies*. Manila (R117-87).
[67] For ADF lending, a limit on country lending of 22.5% was set during the ADF VI replenishment.

the first loan under the revised program lending policy with a $150 million Non-Oil Export Promotion Program loan to Indonesia.[68] The loan supported Indonesia's policies to stimulate non-oil exports. These policies are part of a continuing trend toward deregulation and liberalization with a greater role for the private sector.

Further amendments to the program lending instrument were made in 1996.[69] By then, it was recognized that meeting loan conditions did not guarantee the realization of the expected impact of a program. Even the reformulated program loans tended to be implemented over a relatively short period, providing inadequate time for policies to fully work. Given the significant role of the International Monetary Fund and World Bank in policy-based lending at the macroeconomic level, it was felt that ADB program lending should be strengthened at the sector level. Hence a new sector development program was introduced as a combination of three existing modalities (program loan, project loan, and TA) to address sector needs more comprehensively. Sector analysis became a precondition for program lending. In addition, poverty, social, environmental, and mitigation measures were emphasized.

2.   Special Interventions Project Loan

Another lending facility was introduced for the first time in 1990, with the approval of a $10.5 million Special Interventions Project Loan for Papua New Guinea.[70] Part of a multidonor effort, the loan was intended to mitigate some of the possible social costs of the government structural adjustment programs. Projects to be implemented with the loan, under the Government Public Investment Program, had to have a strong poverty focus and funds had to be disbursed quickly to contain unemployment or income reduction.

3.   Scholarship Program

In its commitment to broaden its beneficiary base, ADB adopted a new operational instrument for education and training—the scholarship program. Two such programs were approved in 1988. The Japan Scholarship Program financed by the Government of Japan provided for postgraduate studies in development-related fields at a number of selected regional institutions for DMC nationals. The Scholarship Program for Smaller DMCs (financed through a regional technical assistance worth $300,000) sponsored short-term scholarships in specific fields of training for candidates nominated by the governments of Bhutan, the Lao PDR, Maldives, and eight Pacific DMCs.

4.   Disaster Emergency Assistance

ADB was the first regional multilateral development bank to adopt a disaster and emergency assistance policy in 1987, with a focus on Pacific countries (Box 10).[71] The policy allowed ADB to assist small DMCs in quickly restoring vital economic infrastructure and social services following damages caused by natural disasters. Through the policy, the Bank was able to provide emergency assistance loans (up to $500,000) under expedited procedures (within 6 weeks of receiving such loan request) and applied its procurement and disbursement procedures more liberally. Initially, this applied only to Maldives, Papua New Guinea, and the small Pacific DMCs given that these DMCs suffer disproportionately from natural disasters. Faced with increasingly disruptive effects of natural and man-made disasters on economic development in many other DMCs, ADB expanded the policy in 1989 to include attention to disaster risk management and the restoration of productive activity for all DMCs.[72] The 1989 policy was significant as it incorporated elements of disaster

---

[68]   ADB. 1987. *Report and Recommendation of the President to the Board of Directors: Proposed Loan to Indonesia for the Non-Oil Export Promotion Program*. Manila (Loans 0876 and 0877).

[69]   ADB. 1996. *Review of the Bank's Program Lending Policies*. Manila.

[70]   ADB. 1990. *Report and Recommendation of the President to the Board of Directors: Proposed Loan to Papua New Guinea for the Special Interventions Project*. Manila (Loan 1054).

[71]   ADB. 1987. *Rehabilitation Assistance to Small DMCs Affected by Natural Disasters*. Manila.

[72]   ADB. 1989. *Rehabilitation Assistance after Disasters*. Manila.

> **Box 10: Disaster Policy and ADB's Response During the Decade**
>
> The Asian Development Bank's (ADB's) early support for rehabilitation assistance for Pacific developing member countries (DMCs) affected by natural disasters included an emergency power rehabilitation assistance to Samoa when Cyclone Ofa struck two major islands (Upolo and Savaii) in 1990; an emergency typhoon rehabilitation assistance program in the Marshall Islands following the destruction of infrastructure and crops by Typhoon Gay in 1992; emergency rehabilitation of the main infrastructure facilities in Solomon Islands after Cyclone Nina in 1993; and emergency support to repair severe damages to infrastructure after the 1994 volcanic eruptions in the town of Rabaul in Papua New Guinea.
>
> In 1991, a devastating cyclone struck Bangladesh, and ADB provided immediate assistance for the repair and rehabilitation of damaged infrastructure through a reallocation of $40 million saved from four ADB-financed projects in the country. In the same year, two natural disasters hit the Philippines. The volcanic eruption of Mt. Pinatubo and the subsequent mudflows resulted in widespread damage to infrastructure and agriculture, a considerable loss of life, and the dislocation of families. In response, ADB provided advisory services to assess the damage followed by emergency assistance to support rehabilitation and recovery plans for affected areas. Later in the year, the Philippines experienced extensive loss of life and property in Leyte (central part of the Philippines) due to Typhoon Uring. ADB quickly provided support for the reconstruction of public facilities in affected areas.
>
> The 1990s saw a growing recognition among the international community of the need to mitigate the effects of natural hazards before they develop into disasters. In 1989, ADB's first disaster-related regional technical assistance led to the dissemination of important disaster management information in two books. The first book summarized lessons learned in selected DMCs, with a focus on overall strategies for disaster mitigation and technological and management issues. The second, essentially a handbook, summarized state-of-the-art disaster management techniques for practitioners in DMCs. These books are among ADB's bestsellers and are still in demand, as references in the field and as text for university and training courses throughout the region.
>
> Sources: ADB. 1989. *Regional Technical Assistance for Regional Study on Disaster Mitigation*. Manila; ADB. 1990. *Disaster Mitigation in Asia and the Pacific*. Manila; ADB. 1991. *Disaster Management: A Disaster Manager's Handbook*. Manila; ADB. 2004. *ADB's Disaster and Emergency Assistance Policy*. Manila; ADB. 2012. *Special Evaluation Study: ADB's Response to Natural Disasters and Disaster Risks*. Manila.

risk reduction. For the first time, ADB explicitly helped DMCs reduce their vulnerability to natural hazards. The new policy also identified ways to prevent disasters or mitigate their effects after they had occurred, allowing DMCs to reallocate surplus funds from other projects to respond to an emergency, provided that the projects were in the same sector. It also expanded the coverage of ADB's disaster assistance policy to include non-natural disaster (e.g., wars, civil strife, and environmental degradation).

B. Project and Loan Administration

More emphasis was given to improving project quality, as projects grew more complex. A major endeavor to enhance the overall delivery of Bank services was initiated in 1993 with the setting up of the Task Force on Improving Project Quality, chaired by VP Schulz. Although it was essentially an in-house effort, the task force interacted with DMCs and also benefited from the views of two external experts (both former executive directors of the Bank). The report of the task force was one of the most important policy papers reviewed by the Board in 1994.[73] It identified three major themes or areas of focus to improve project quality and impact.

First, ADB needed to pay greater attention to the needs of its DMCs. This implied shifting away from an "approval culture" in which adequate project design and attention to local needs, demands, and absorptive capacity were sacrificed to achieve annual lending targets. It also meant strengthening the country focus

---

[73] ADB. 1994. *Report of the Task Force on Improving Project Quality*. Manila.

of operations, including the links between economic and sector work, programming, and project design. Second, ADB needed to put more emphasis on the development of institutional capacity and on country ownership. This required stronger long-term programs in DMCs and involvement of DMC officials and beneficiaries at all stages of the project cycle. Third, there should be more accountability within the Bank for ensuring project quality. To do this, project implementation should be given the same priority as project processing. The report recommended a one-time "spring cleaning" of the project portfolio to weed out inactive and slow-moving projects. In addition, systems and procedures should be more decentralized to allow greater flexibility and initiative, and feedback from lessons of past experiences should be better utilized in the design and implementation of projects and programs. An action plan was developed to implement the report's recommendations. As a result, a review of ADB's organizational set-up was also completed to ensure a strengthened country focus in operations. A new organizational structure dividing the Bank under two "regionalized" Vice-Presidents (East and West) became effective in 1995.

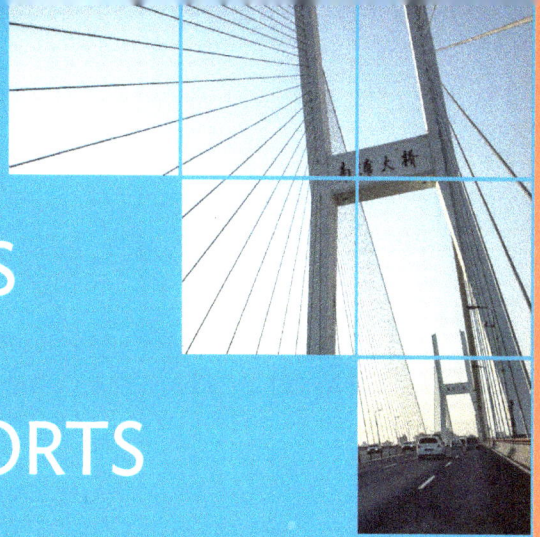

VI. FINANCIAL POLICIES AND RESOURCE MOBILIZATION EFFORTS

- ADB remained actively engaged in resource mobilization efforts. Preparatory work started for a fourth general capital increase, which would take over 8 years to complete. There were two rounds of Asian Development Fund replenishments.
- In parallel, ADB introduced numerous enhancements to its financial management practices to retain the Bank's "AAA" rating in the capital markets, which underpinned ADB's ability to raise low-cost, competitive funding that it could then extend to developing member countries.

A. Ordinary Capital Resources

At the close of the third decade (31 December 1996), the Bank's authorized capital stock amounted to $50.1 billion (compared to $19.7 billion at the end of the second decade).[74] This included subscriptions from the fourth general capital increase (GCI IV) and earlier GCIs; subscriptions from nine new members; and special capital increases for Japan, Sweden, and the United States (US) (approved by the Board of Governors in 1988).

1. Fourth General Capital Increase

In May 1986, at the request of the Board of Governors, ADB initiated a study of its future resource requirements, which would eventually lead to the formulation of specific proposals for GCI IV, whose negotiations lasted until May 1994. As part of the negotiations, ADB undertook a series of studies on its income and liquidity policies and its loan charges.

---

[74] This section draws heavily from ADB. 2016. *A History of Financial Management at the Asian Development Bank*. Manila.

Ongoing Review of Financial Policies. In considering the need for a GCI and the target date by which countries should make their subscription, ADB normally took into account (i) the limitation imposed by the ADB Charter on ordinary lending operations, (ii) the limitation on borrowing imposed by certain covenants in bond issues, and (iii) other limitations on financial activities arising from general considerations of prudent financial management.

Lending Limitation. Article 12.1 of the ADB Charter states that the total amount of outstanding loans, equity investment, and guarantees in ordinary operations should not at any time exceed the total amount of its subscribed capital and ordinary reserve (known as the Bank's lending authority). In the past, the Charter reference to "amount of outstanding loans" had been interpreted as the total amount of loan commitments, net of repayments (also referred to as net loan commitments). The difference between the lending limitation and the volume of net loan commitments is known as the Bank's lending headroom, which measures the Bank's financial ability to commit additional loans. A GCI would normally be required before the headroom reaches zero, to avoid a hiatus in the Bank's lending activities.

The International Bank for Reconstruction and Development (IBRD) had similar charter limitations on lending but interpreted them differently—in terms of loans disbursed and not yet repaid (rather than in terms of loans committed, which included the undisbursed portions of loans). During the GCI IV negotiation discussions, ADB considered adopting a similar approach, as it would provide for additional headroom. However, after lengthy discussions, ADB ultimately opted to maintain the traditional interpretation since this had been the practice to date and was considered the closest interpretation to the original intention of the Charter. ADB's decision was consistent with the institution's cautious approach toward financial management.[75]

Borrowing Limitation. In the past, and as a result of covenants included in earlier bond issues, the Bank's borrowings had been restricted to the callable capital subscribed by specified member countries whose currencies are convertible (this covenant was known as the callable capital in convertible currencies limit or "CCCC limit." In previous GCIs, this limit had been the main factor triggering the need for a capital increase and determining its timing. During the GCI IV negotiations, however, only one such borrowing was still outstanding and projected to mature by June 1993. The Board agreed to redeem it and redefine its borrowing limitation policy to remove the callable capital in convertible currencies limit, thereby increasing the Bank's borrowing capacity substantially. As a result, and unlike in previous GCIs, the Bank's lending limitation became the primary consideration in determining the size and timing of GCI IV.

Other Limitation Policies. The Bank also had a policy of maintaining its year-end holdings of liquid assets at no less than 40% of undisbursed balances of both effective and not yet effective loans. The Bank's primary objective in holding liquidity at this level was to ensure the uninterrupted availability of funds for its operations, while maintaining flexibility in its borrowing decisions, in case of adverse conditions in the capital markets.

In September 1987, the Bank sought to maintain the adequacy of its net income by ensuring that its long-term interest-coverage ratio would not fall substantially below 1.25, while the minimum target for the Bank's long-term reserves to outstanding loan ratio would be maintained within the range of 20%–25%.[76] Certain reductions in loan charges were also approved, providing significant cost savings to borrowing member countries.

---

[75] During parallel GCI negotiations, similar considerations took place at the Inter-American Development Bank, which eventually opted to adopt IBRD's interpretation.
[76] The interest-coverage ratio measures ability to meet its debt obligations out of earnings. The reserves to outstanding loan ratio measures the ability to protect itself against capital impairment due to possible loan losses.

A comprehensive review of ADB's investment guidelines was undertaken in 1991. The objective of the review was to enhance ADB's flexibility in meeting its income objectives, while retaining its sound risk management practices. Essentially, the existing guidelines were split into two parts: the Investment Authority dealing with overall investment policy to be approved by the Board of Directors; and the Investment Guidelines, providing detailed guidance and relevant limits to be applied to the actual management of the portfolio, to be approved by Management. The benefits from the new Investment Authority were expected to be significant. Futures and option contracts would allow the Bank to change the risk profile of its investment portfolio quickly without disturbing its cash market security positions, enhance the liquidity of certain higher-yielding investments, and lower transaction costs.

Financial policies were further reviewed in 1992. An interdepartmental working group was established to review the country risks of the Bank's loan portfolio and portfolio concentration. In response, ADB committed to diversify its portfolio and strengthen its country risk assessment and management systems. An explicit policy was adopted for loan sanctions, loan loss provisioning, along with a new policy framework for its private sector operations to minimize the impact of such operations on the overall OCR portfolio risk. The Bank also approved in parallel new currency management practices to improve the currency composition of the borrower's debt obligations relative to the applicable lending rate and the predictability of their debt service repayments. This was in response to shareholders' concerns, given the debt crisis faced in other regions of the world. The review also included a further review of the Bank's liquidity policy, income management policy, and major financial indicators (interest-coverage ratio and reserves to outstanding loan ratio). While the Bank adopted a cash flow approach in its liquidity management, no changes were made to its income management policies. Finally, the Board gave preliminary considerations to the paid-in capital requirements for GCI IV.

In early 1994, ADB started an annual income review to assess its medium-term income prospects. The review was meant to assess the Bank's ability to meet its Board-approved income policy objectives, taking into account the various financial risks facing the Bank. On the basis of this annual review, the Board would review the adequacy of loan charges and would recommend to the Board of Governors how net income should be allocated. This process is still being implemented to date.

An initial proposal for GCI IV was considered by the Board in November 1993. Management projected that the Bank's lending headroom would be nearly exhausted by the end of 1993. The Board generally agreed on the need for a further GCI in the range of 100%–120%. This was envisaged to support OCR operations growing at an average of 7.7%–10.5% annually over a 6-year period. The future role of the Bank and its operational agenda were key factors for consideration in finalizing GCI IV. In line with the recommendations in the Panel Report on the Bank's Role in the 1990s,[77] Management committed to (i) further strengthen its recently adopted strategic planning process and adopt a broad-based development approach and country focus, through improvements in its organizational structure, business processes, staff incentives, and expertise; (ii) strengthen its environmental activities; (iii) pay particular attention to social dimensions in operations; (iv) revise key sector policies; (v) give increased attention to population issues; (vi) implement fully the recently revised financial policies; (vii) further improve interagency collaboration and aid coordination; (viii) prepare an issues paper on good governance, formulate new policies on disclosure of operational information, and examine how the Bank can best respond to issues relating to its inspection function (following similar developments at the World Bank); and (ix) seek closer working relationship with members of the Board on operational matters and develop stronger partnership with DMCs to improve project quality and implementation.

[77] See also section III.A.

After the initial proposal in 1993, the Board submitted in early 1994 its final recommendation to the Board of Governors for a substantial increase in the Bank's authorized and subscribed capital stock of 100%. On 22 May, the Board of Governors authorized it. GCI IV became effective immediately (on the same day) and amounted to almost 1.8 million shares worth over $25 billion (Table 3). Subscriptions were to consist of a 2% paid-in portion, with the remaining 98% in the form of callable shares. Of the payments for the paid-in shares, 40% were to be in convertible currency and 60% in the national currency of the subscribing member. The final date of subscription was set to 31 December 1995. The deadline was subsequently extended by 6 months to 30 June 1996 and by a further 3 months until 30 September 1996. Fifty-five members had subscribed by the final deadline. Italy and the Philippines would be late in making their payments and, as a result, their voting power had to be temporarily reduced.

Table 3: General Capital Increases and Capital Composition, 1966–1994

	Initial Subscription (1966)	GCI I (1971)	GCI II (1976)	GCI III (1983)	GCI IV (1994)
Capital Increase					
% increase	0	150	135	105	100
Number of new shares	110,000	165,000	414,800	754,750	1,770,497
Composition of Capital (%)					
Callable	50	80	90	95	98
Paid-in	50	20	10	5	2
Components of Paid-in Capital (%)					
Convertible currency	50	40	40	40	40
National currency	50	60	60	60	60

GCI = general capital increase.
Note: Increases in authorized capital are based on the number of subscribed shares, which may be lower than the number of authorized shares.
Source: Asian Development Bank.

2. Borrowings

As the Bank's lending operations grew, and with the need to maintain its liquidity target, paid-in capital continued to be supplemented with borrowings. Total borrowings doubled in the third decade to $12.2 billion (against $6.4 billion in the previous decade). About half of total borrowings were from Japan and Eurobond markets. The Bank also placed bond issuances in the global market, including Austria, Germany, the Netherlands, Switzerland, and the US; and Asian markets including Hong Kong, China; the Republic of Korea; and Taipei,China.

The Bank's borrowing program has evolved over the years. In the first decade, the main concern was to become known in as many markets as possible and to maintain a regular presence in them. In the second decade, when interest rates started to rise, the Bank was compelled to concentrate its borrowing in low-interest currency. The third stage came with the Bank's introduction of a pool-based variable lending rate in 1986. It came at a time when globalization and deregulation were sweeping world capital markets. Under this system, the Bank was able to concentrate its borrowing in low-coupon currencies, but by using financial engineering techniques such as swaps, it was able to expand in high-coupon markets.

The Bank also made conscious efforts to stimulate the development of Asian's markets. This was best exemplified in the "Dragon Bond" concept that ADB started. The first Dragon Bond issue (worth $300 million) was launched in 1991 simultaneously in the capital markets of Hong Kong, China; Singapore; and Taipei,China. This pioneering example demonstrated ADB's significant understanding of the regional bond market at that time and would be replicated by a series of top-rated issuers, such as international and regional financial institutions in Europe and the US. A second Dragon Bond issue followed in October 1992. This was the first borrowing for the Bank's newly established pool-based, variable rate, US dollar-specific lending window. In the following year, the Bank issued its first ever Dragon yen bond issue, providing it with an opportunity to diversify its cost-effective sources of yen funding and at the same time, introduce another international currency to the Asian regional bond market. During this period, the Bank continued to focus on enhancing the secondary market liquidity of its bonds through targeted and sizable benchmark issuance in selected markets. The move toward large benchmark issues accelerated in 1994 and 1995, with the first two US dollar "global" bonds (bonds issued in several countries at the same time and traded outside the country where the currency is denominated) ever issued by the Bank.

3. Market-Based Window, Cofinancing, and Guarantee Operations

In light of the growing need of DMCs for capital, the limited volume of official development assistance, and the resulting need for an increased mobilization of private resources, ADB introduced its market-based loan window and reviewed its cofinancing and guarantee strategy.

In 1994, the Board approved the establishment of a new market-based loan window to provide funds at current terms prevailing in international capital markets,[78] which became the Bank's third lending window.[79] The new window primarily benefited the private sector and broadened the product

line offered by the Bank, with access limited to financial intermediaries in the public sector and all borrowers in the private sector.

ADB also continued to pursue its efforts as a catalyst to increase resource flows to DMCs through cofinancing and guarantee operations. In 1988, the Bank approved a policy framework to guarantee loans by private sector institutions to DMCs.[80] The framework was approved in light of substantial balance-of-payments surpluses in some DMCs combined with difficulties in mobilizing sufficient resource flows on acceptable terms to sustain economic recovery programs. The guarantees were to be used only in selected circumstances on a case-by-case basis. ADB's guarantee facility was used for the first time in Indonesia in 1989.

Cofinancing operations gained momentum with the approval of new cofinancing and guarantee policies in 1995. The main objectives of the new cofinancing strategy were to catalyze additional private capital to DMCs by assisting cofinanciers in the appraisal and management of risks, and to continue to promote official cofinancing, particularly for low-income countries.[81] Implementation of the strategy called for the mainstreaming of cofinancing activities in Bank operations. The Office of Cofinancing Operations was established in 1996 for this purpose.

Under its new guarantee policy, the Bank agreed to provide either a credit guarantee, providing all-inclusive cover for a portion of the debt service; or a risk guarantee, covering specific risk events for all or part of the debt service. The eligibility criteria for guarantee operations were also enlarged.[82]

Over the third decade, official cofinancing continued to account for the largest share of cofinancing arrangements. Direct value-added

---

[78] ADB. 1994. *A Proposal to Introduce a Market-Based Loan Window*. Manila.
[79] The other two windows were pool-based multicurrency loan window, and pool-based single currency loan window in US dollars.
[80] ADB. 1987. *Bank's Guarantee Operations*. Manila.
[81] ADB. 1995. *The Bank's Cofinancing Strategy*. Manila.
[82] Previously, the Cofinancing Unit, which was created in March 1982, served as the focal point for official and commercial cofinancing. ADB. 1994. *Review of the Bank's Guarantee Operations*. Manila.

(DVA) cofinancing[83] from official sources (bilateral and multilateral donors) increased to $3.9 billion covering 54 loan and grant projects (compared to $499 million for 50 projects in the previous decade). The Japan Bank for International Cooperation was the top source, accounting for over 90% of official DVA cofinancing. Other sources included the International Fund for Agricultural Development, the OPEC Fund for International Development, Frankfurt-based KfW Development Bank, the Netherlands, the International Bank for Reconstruction and Development, Norway, and the International Cooperation and Development Fund. Cofinanced loans were most prominently used for large infrastructure projects in energy, transport and ICT, agriculture, and water and other municipal infrastructure services. In addition, the Bank actively pursued TA cofinancing. TA cofinancing from external sources almost doubled in value compared to the previous decade (reaching $132 million and covering 171 TA projects.)

B.   Special Funds and Facilities

1.   The Japan Special Fund

At the 20th Annual Meeting of the Bank in Osaka, the Government of Japan expressed interest in establishing a special fund to contribute to the accelerated economic growth of the Bank's DMCs. The Japan Special Fund was formally established in March 1988. It aimed to support DMCs' efforts toward industrialization, natural and human resource development, and technology transfer, and was to be used to finance or cofinance (i) TA projects (on a grant basis) in both public and private sectors, including project preparation, advisory services, and regional activities; (ii) private sector development projects through equity investment; and (iii) in special cases and on a grant basis, TA components of Bank-financed public sector development projects. The Fund had an initial contribution of 2.5 billion yen (equivalent to about $20 million) on 25 March 1988, supplemented by a further contribution of 2 billion yen ($16 million)

a month later. Annual contributions peaked in 1995 with just over $100 million. From 1990, the Japan Special Fund was diversified to support specific activities (economic and research work, environment-related activities, gender activities, and others). Proposals were submitted at regular intervals. A small unit was established in ADB to process this work and that required for other Japanese funds. Annual administration costs were charged to the Japan Special Fund.

2.   Fifth Replenishment of ADF (ADF VI: 1992–1995)

With the ADF V period scheduled to conclude at the end of 1990, a meeting of representatives of ADF donor countries was held at the time of the 23rd Annual Meeting in May 1990 in New Delhi to consider the ADF resource position and the timeframe for a further ADF replenishment (ADF VI). Additional meetings were held in September 1990 in Washington, DC; January 1991 in Tokyo; April 1991 in Vancouver; June 1991 in Stockholm; September 1991 in Istanbul; and December 1991 in London. At these meetings, donors reiterated their support for ADF and discussed various matters relating to the replenishment.

In January 1991, the Board completed a review of ADF financial policies and made three key decisions. One, ADB should commence using the ADF investment portfolio for ADF loan disbursements with a view to gradually wind down the portfolio over the period 1991–1995. Two, ADB should discontinue the existing policy of maintaining a provision for exchange rate fluctuations in determining the availability of ADF resources for loan commitments. Instead, ADB should adopt an ADF lending limitation policy in order to reduce the risk of undisbursed resources becoming overcommitted as a result of exchange rate fluctuations. Three, 85% of projected ADF investment income and loan repayments during the period 1991–1995 should be made available to the Bank immediately as advance ADF commitment authority, thereby enabling ADF borrowers to benefit from this growing source of funds at the

---

83   Cofinancing with contractual or collaborative arrangements between ADB and financing partners.

earliest possible date. As a result of these policy changes (particularly the third item), additional ADF resources of about $1.5 billion became available in early 1991. Consequently, donors agreed at the Tokyo meeting that commencement of the ADF VI period should be delayed by a year, to cover 1992–1995.

During the various meetings, several major policy issues were discussed. These covered not only the directions that ADF operations should take over the ADF V period, but also specific operational aspects and suggestions for strengthening planning and management systems within the institution. More specifically, donors urged ADB to (i) give higher priority to poverty and social sector issues in its operations; (ii) strengthen its efforts to support policy reforms in its DMCs through more thorough economic and sector analysis, TA, and lending operations; (iii) integrate fully environmental activities into its overall operations; (iv) pay greater attention to the effects of ADB projects on women and the need to enhance women's opportunities to contribute and benefit from economic development; and (v) increase assistance for activities designed to address population problems. Donors also highlighted the need to strengthen the Bank's strategic planning capability and country programming process, as well as the need to enhance social sector investments and attention to cross-cutting issues, including women in development, poverty reduction, the environment, and private sector development. They requested that an overall review of the Bank's organizational structure be undertaken.

Donors also underlined the importance of establishing a link between the allocation of ADF resources to individual DMCs and the effective use of such resources, as was increasingly being done by the International Development Association (IDA). ADB was asked to emphasize performance as a criterion for allocating ADF resources to individual DMCs. Country performance should be assessed regularly (annually or biennially) in

terms of sound economic management, efforts toward growth with equity and poverty reduction, and efforts toward sustainable economic and social development. Given the continued needs of traditional ADF recipients and other potential borrowers,[84] donors concluded that it would not be possible to make ADF resources available to the PRC and India during the ADF IV period (even though both of them were classified as Group A countries and hence eligible). Indonesia and the Philippines were two Group B countries that were granted renewed access to ADF resources on a temporary basis during ADF V, to assist through major economic restructuring efforts. Donors allowed the possibility of continued but reduced ADF access for those two countries during ADF VI for projects directed at poverty reduction, social sectors, and protection of the environment.

The ADF VI negotiations were concluded in December 1991. Donors eventually agreed on a total replenishment size of $4.2 billion (2.969 billion in special drawing rights). Of this amount, $140 million was to be set aside and allocated to the Technical Assistance Special Fund primarily for project-related TA to poorer DMCs or for regional TA. Donors also recommended that the BOD consider annually the use of OCR income for the financing of technical operations. Notwithstanding this, the existing policy of receiving voluntary Technical Assistance Special Fund contributions from member countries would continue. Most donors contributed based on the burden sharing arrangement of ADF V except for the Republic of Korea and Sweden that substantially increased their contributions. Nauru; Taipei,China; and Turkey participated in the replenishment negotiations for the first time. Hong Kong, China and Finland made additional contributions; while Denmark, Japan, the Netherlands, Spain, Switzerland, and the United Kingdom provided supplementary contributions. Japan and Australia reduced their burden share contributions to around 33.7% (Japan's original burden share) and 6.5%, respectively. The ADF VI arrangements became effective on 20 August 1992, when the total

---

[84] Potential borrowers consisted of three DMCs in which the Bank had no lending program for many years (Afghanistan, Cambodia, and Viet Nam); Myanmar (which did not borrow from ADB during ADF V); new members that recently joined the Bank (the Marshall Islands, the Federated States of Micronesia, and Mongolia); and potential new members from Central Asia.

amount of unqualified commitments received by the Bank reached $2.1 billion (or 50% of total committed amount).

3. Sixth Replenishment of ADF (ADF VII: 1997–2000)

As an initial step, donors held an informal consultation in May 1995 in Auckland to review ADF operations and resources. As the ADF commitment authority was nearing exhaustion, donors agreed to formally start negotiations on a further ADF replenishment (ADF VII) to finance the Bank's concessional operations over the period 1997–2000.[85] Donors subsequently held seven meetings in Amsterdam in November 1995; Bonn in February 1996; Manila in April 1996; Hong Kong, China in June 1996; Kuala Lumpur in September 1996; Copenhagen in October 1996; and Tokyo in January 1997. All meetings were chaired by President Sato.

During negotiations for the previous replenishment (ADF VI) as well as GCI IV, donors had requested the Bank to reorient its strategic objectives and operational priorities. Donors endorsed the continued validity of these priorities over the ADF VII period and stressed that the emphasis should now shift to effectively implementing the policy and operational changes introduced so far. While stressing the continued relevance of the strategic agenda and objectives resulting from ADF VI and GCI IV, donors noted that the global and regional contexts were substantially different from those of previous replenishments. Concessional resources were very scarce and the role and expectations of multilateral development finance had changed considerably. In this context, donors outlined their long-term vision to make ADF operations progressively self-financing.

To ensure continued support to ADF, traditional donors indicated that they would need to be assured that their level of contributions would gradually decrease over time. This would require the integration of donor resource mobilization

efforts and effective financial management on one hand, and accelerated development and graduation from concessional assistance on the other. In augmenting the volume of nondonor resources, two approaches were considered: OCR net income transfer to ADF and hardening of ADF loan terms. Donors requested ADB to undertake a comprehensive review of its financial policies, in order to develop a new planning framework for the financial management of ADF resources. Other general policies relating to ADF should also be developed and/or reviewed, such as access criteria, lending terms, graduation, performance evaluation, and resource allocation.

Donors also emphasized the need for broadening the base for donor resources. In this context, traditional donors recognized and appreciated the Bank's efforts to mobilize donor support, through consultations with nonborrower DMCs and advanced borrower DMCs within the region. Donors agreed that the overall burden share between nonregional and regional donors should move from 55:45 under ADF VI toward parity. Ultimately, donors agreed to an ADF VII lending program of $6.3 billion, of which $2.6 million was expected to be generated from donor contributions. Japan agreed to a higher burden share of 35.1%. Several higher-income borrowing developing members such as Hong Kong, China; the Republic of Korea; and Taipei,China increased their contributions significantly. Malaysia and Thailand became new donors. As a result, the burden share between nonregional and regional donors (including supplementary contributions) reached 49.4:49.1. The near parity between nonregional and regional members in total donor contributions was considered a major milestone. ADF VII became effective on 24 September 1997, when the total amount of unqualified contribution received by the Bank exceeded the minimum trigger. Contributions were to become available to the Bank for operational commitments in four equal tranches over 1997–2000.

---

85 At the end of 1995, the maximum amount of new lending that the Bank could undertake with available ADF resources was about $1.4 billion. By end 1996, this amount was projected to drop to $400 million.

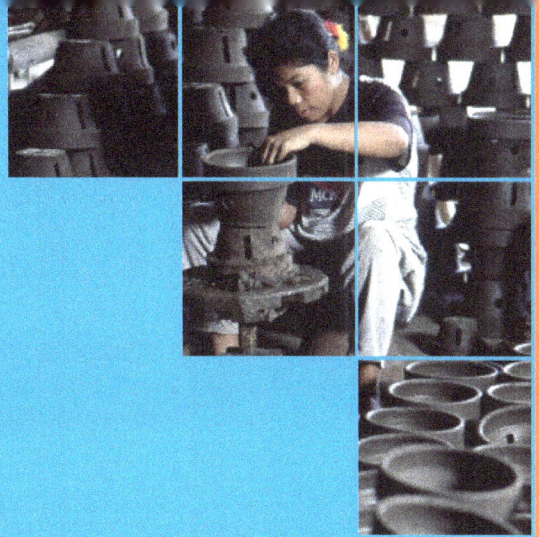

VII. KEY LESSONS FROM EVALUATION

- Given the growth in lending operations and the rapid increase in the number of completed projects, ADB switched in 1988 from a policy of postevaluating all completed projects to one of selective postevaluation of projects.
- ADB began to play an increasing role in helping DMCs develop and strengthen their own evaluation capabilities.

The postevaluation program of ADB had been run by the Post-Evaluation Office (PEO), which reported directly to the President and had two main objectives: to improve the design, implementation and performance of future development projects in light of past experience; and to enable the Bank to better account for the effectiveness of its assistance. Postevaluation was generally carried out 3–4 years after a project was implemented to ensure availability of adequate data relating to project costs and benefits to facilitate a more objective assessment of project performance and sustainability. Project performance audit reports examined the effectiveness and sustainability of projects and focused on specific issues meriting closer attention. Apart from project performance audit reports, PEO also conducted impact evaluations, reevaluations, and special studies.[86]

From 1987 to 1996, PEO completed 299 project performance audit reports, 19 technical assistance performance audit reports, 13 impact evaluation reports, 24 reevaluation studies, and 15 special studies.

The Audit Committee of the Board was responsible for reviewing the work of PEO at the time and for ensuring that lessons learned from the experience of completed projects were properly taken into account in the design of new projects. In 1987, the Board committees were rationalized. The audit and budget review committees were expanded to six members each, while the committee for administrative matters relating to Members of the Board was disbanded.[87] In the same year, the audit committee advised that an additional project category *unsatisfactory* should be added to the category of *generally successful* and *partially*

---

[86] Impact evaluation and reevaluation studies took a second look at projects on the basis of a sufficiently long period to assess actual benefits (including lasting contributions in a DMC's development) and reassess their economic and technical viabilities. Special studies involved intensive analysis of a particular issue of operational importance in a specific country, sector, or region.

[87] Prior to being disbanded, this committee was responsible for reviewing the provisions for shipment allowances and insurance on appointment, termination, and official travel for members of the Board.

successful.[88] Of the 299 projects and programs evaluated over the decade, 53% were rated *generally successful*, 35% *partially successful*, and 12% *unsuccessful*. Projects in the energy, industry, and transport and ICT sectors had higher success rates. In contrast, projects in the agriculture and social infrastructure sectors did not perform as well.

Given the growth in the Bank's lending operations and the rapid increase in the number of completed projects, ADB switched in 1988 from a policy of postevaluation of completed projects to one of selective postevaluation of projects, while evaluating all program and sector loans. This helped release PEO's limited resources to initiate new activities, such as postevaluation of TA and strengthening the evaluation capacity of DMCs. In 1988, PEO undertook, for the first time, in-depth evaluations of TA projects (i.e., a project preparation TA in Indonesia and an advisory TA project in Solomon Islands). Over the decade, lessons from technical assistance performance audit reports included the need for carefully preparing the terms of reference for consultants and recruiting consultants with good knowledge of local conditions). The need to accurately assess the effective demand for services and the absorptive capacity of beneficiary agencies was also identified, as were ensuring high levels of TA ownership by the government and recipient agency, hands-on TA management, and intensive supervision of TA consultants. Toward the end of the decade and in line with the recommendations of the task force on improving project quality, the postevaluation program placed greater emphasis on impact evaluation studies, reevaluation studies, and special studies.

Building Evaluation Capacity in Developing Member Countries. The Bank also began to play an increasing role in helping DMCs develop and strengthen their own evaluation capabilities. Throughout the decade, PEO organized various activities (such as trainings and seminars) aimed at increasing the awareness in DMCs of

the importance of performance evaluation as a management and planning tool. In 1992, a regional seminar was organized in Malaysia. One of the main outputs of the seminar was the adoption of an action plan for strengthening performance evaluation in Asia and the Pacific.

Feedback of Postevaluation Findings. Efforts continued to facilitate the application of lessons learned with a view to improve new and ongoing projects. A management committee on post-evaluation findings was established in 1991. It held biannual meetings to discuss issues arising from postevaluation studies that warranted specific attention and guidance from Management. PEO also initiated an internal review of its current feedback system to further improve the dissemination of postevaluation findings. PEO's computerized Post-Evaluation Information System was redesigned in 1995 and became operational in 1996. The system allowed all Bank staff to access PEO reports. These efforts were supplemented by the circulation of postevaluation abstracts, annual review of post-evaluation reports, and country and sector syntheses of postevaluation findings (see Box 11).

One of the recommendations of the task force on improving project quality was that the Bank should prepare each year a comprehensive annual performance evaluation program to bring together the activities of various departments and offices as they relate to project performance. The first annual performance evaluation program was issued in 1996, reviewing activities completed in 1995. It concluded that the institutional mechanism for generating feedback in the Bank was fairly comprehensive and well developed. It also noted growing awareness, appreciation, and use of the feedback process among Bank staff, as well as by some DMCs. Nevertheless, some possible improvements were identified at various stages of the project cycle. Some questions were also raised on the level of resources made available for project and TA supervision activities. These were deemed insufficient to implement the recommendations of the task force.

---

[88] A project was considered generally successful if it was expected to be economically viable or could generate socioeconomic benefits commensurate with original expectations and/or costs incurred. A project was rated as *partly successful* if its benefits were believed to be sustainable at reduced levels, with reasonable prospects for improvement if remedial actions were taken. A project was classified as *unsuccessful* if it was not technically or economically viable.

Box 11: Country Synthesis of Postevaluation Findings in the Philippines

Total assistance by the Asian Development Bank (ADB) to the Philippines from 1967 to 1996 had reached $6.2 billion, making the Philippines the third largest recipient of ADB financing after Indonesia and Pakistan. By sector, ADB assistance was broken down as follows: energy (27%), agriculture and agro-industry (25%), social infrastructure (16%), transport and information and communication technology (15%), finance (10%), multisector (5%), and private sector (2%). Fifty percent of postevaluated projects were rated *generally successful*, 26% as *partly successful,* and 24% as *unsuccessful*. These findings caused concerns both for the Philippine government and for ADB. Common factors affecting project performance were (i) inadequate assessment of sector-related institutional and policy issues and macroeconomic conditions in project preparation and appraisal; (ii) poor analysis of risks and uncertainties arising from external forces, domestic policy distortions, natural calamities, and political turmoil; (iii) lack of availability of counterpart funding from the government; and (iv) weak supervision and monitoring feedback mechanisms. Sector-wise, agriculture projects incurred greater incidence of failures given the complexity of scope and multiplicity of project components.

A study by ADB's Post-Evaluation Office offered a number of recommendations to improve project performance. During project preparation, the Bank should not solely focus on technical aspects of creating new infrastructure facilities but should also consider relevant elements to ensure sustainability of operations and continued maintenance of facilities created, and the efficient management of natural resources. Timely availability of counterpart funding should be realistically assessed in country programming exercises, and if the problems were concerned largely with fiscal management, policy dialogue relating to fiscal policy reforms should be pursued with the government. More critical assessments of macroeconomic and market conditions, demand forecasts, input availability, and external risk factors ought to be undertaken and linked with project performance indicators and targets. Beneficiary participation and preferences should also be sought in designing and implementing projects to improve their quality and sustainability. The government and the Bank should also consider a systematic approach to monitor projects during implementation and after completion to sustain their developmental impacts. Finally, the Bank should seek to improve the effectiveness of its technical assistance for institutional strengthening in the Philippines with emphasis on improving the organizational structures of executing agencies, streamlining of procedures, reforming incentive systems, and training staff.

Source: ADB. 1996. *Country Synthesis of Evaluation Findings in the Philippines*. Manila.

VIII. EPILOGUE

Presdent Sato's speech at the 30th Annual Meeting of the Board Governors in May 1997 in Fukuoka summarized well the mood at the end of the third decade (Box 12).

Box 12: Excerpts from President Mitsuo Sato's Speech at the 30th Annual Meeting

The Last 30 Years in Asia—Extraordinary Achievements

Over the last 3 decades, developing Asia has emerged at a speed unparalleled in history, from economic laggard to growth leader. Asia's "flying geese" have elicited wonder and admiration from around the world, and the Asian Development Bank (ADB) has been able to assist in their takeoff. First in the newly industrializing economies, or NIEs, industries were able to capitalize on the dual logic of comparative advantage and competition with spectacular results. Then Southeast Asian countries followed this example, liberalizing their economies and launching into rapid growth. In this way, the lives of hundreds of millions were improved. ADB learned many valuable lessons by contributing to this development, lessons that have since then been incorporated in our programs for other countries. Following basically the same pattern, the People's Republic of China, Viet Nam, and other Asian transitional economies implemented wide-ranging reforms, and the Bank supported their efforts. Reduction of state intervention followed in South Asia and ADB assisted the reform process there too. Asian governments played an active role in promoting and coordinating economic activity, especially in the earlier stages of growth. To enhance the productivity of labor, they ensured broad access to education, housing, and other public services. They provided crucial infrastructure and encouraged the region's entrepreneurial spirit.

ADB Achievements

The Bank has been an integral player in this transformation. ADB has acquired broad multidisciplinary expertise and a strong record of operational performance over the past 30 years. This is recognized by its member countries, as reflected in the recent successful conclusion of the sixth Asian Development Fund replenishment. Asia's NIEs, whose development was assisted by the Bank, actively participated in the replenishment. This testifies to Asian solidarity. Along with the traditional donors, their participation also demonstrates the continued relevance of multilateralism and the confidence and trust that all shareholders have in the Bank to carry out its development mandate. The growth of annual lending volume reveals only a small segment of the Bank's overall role in the historical transformation that has taken place in Asia. More importantly, ADB has assisted developing member countries (DMCs) though policy reforms, by helping build institutional capacity, by disseminating best practices, and by inspiring DMCs to develop.

This confidence and trust we have gained is the result of having closely worked in partnership with our DMCs. We are attuned to their changing needs and emerging development constraints. We listen before we speak. We diagnose before we prescribe. And we continue to make follow-up. In short, we are the family doctor.

continued.

Box 12. continued.

The confidence and trust we have gained is also the result of the Bank's concern about efficiency and effectiveness. ADB monitors carefully the quality of its projects, and is very conscious of the need to improve operational efficiency. We pay close attention to the management of staff and budgetary resources, and exercise prudence is seeking additional resources. ADB is thus recognized as one of the most efficient development institutions. The Bank is proving itself as a living institution. We have been striving to adapt to the changing needs and emerging challenges of the region, and to the changing ideas as development thinking progresses, just as dynamic Asian economies have displayed an extraordinary ability to adapt.

Looking to the Future

Looking ahead, we see the trend toward global economic interdependence on an ever increasing scale. The future of a particular economy will depend not only on its own circumstances; it will also be linked to the global economy. We see the rising tide of private capital flows across borders, far surpassing official development assistance in the developing world. Harnessing private capital for the purpose of more productive investment has become a major task facing DMCs. Official development assistance will have to expand its role from mere resource transfers to catalyzing continued development on a broad front. In country after country, we see the process of economic reforms and institutional changes taking place. Striking a more synergetic balance between market and state is now essential. Amid all this change, however, poverty persists. Tremendous social issues are compounded by environmental degradation.

Against this background, the Bank has reshaped its strategic agenda. I believe four areas constitute the most important entry points to exert our development efforts: (i) to intensify our efforts in poverty reduction; (ii) to facilitate policy and institutional reforms, especially for economies in transition; (iii) to raise productivity, particularly in middle income countries to ensure continued economic dynamism; and (iv) to promote subregional cooperation, not only to accelerate the growth momentum but also to maintain and ensure peace and stability. By combining policy support, capacity building, promotion of regional cooperation, and highly selective and leveraged project financing, ADB aims to maximize its overall development impact. This is the type of multilateral assistance called for in this new era of the region's development. And this is also where we have a comparative advantage vis-à-vis other development agencies and the private sector.

Conclusion

The region's and the Bank's progress over the last 30 years is highly encouraging. But formidable challenges remain, which the Bank is relevant to address.

In closing, therefore, permit me to quote what the Bank's founding President, Mr. Takeshi Watanabe, wrote in his memoirs, *Towards a New Asia*, some 24 years ago. "All people harbor dreams...in my capacity as the first president of the ADB, I was able to be personally involved in the process in which this new international organization took shape as realization of my dream...it is a particular source of satisfaction for me to know that it was a dream that has brought happiness to hundreds of millions of people. However, what has been accomplished to date is only part of the great dream. I shall continue to dream, confident that those who will follow me will continue to join hands in their efforts to see that the whole of this dream comes true."

Let us join hands and work together to make the whole of this great dream come true.

Source: ADB. 1997. Opening Address. Speech by President Mitsuo Sato delivered at the 30th Annual Meeting of the ADB Board of Governors. Fukuoka. 11–13 May 1997.

APPENDIXES

Appendix Table A1.1: Key Macroeconomic Indicators, 1986 and 1996

	GDP (2010 constant US$, million)		Population (million)		GDP per capita (2010 constant US$)		Agriculture (%)		Share in GDP Industry (%)		Services (%)	
	1986	1996	1986	1996	1986	1996	1986	1996	1986	1996	1986	1996
Central and West Asia	...	213,618	167.8	212.3	...	1,097	28	24	23	27	49	49
Afghanistan	...	...	11.4	17.5	...	...	...	38 (2002)	...	24	...	38 (2002)
Armenia	...	3,554	3.4	3.2	...	1,120	17 (1990)	37	52 (1990)	33	31 (1990)	31
Azerbaijan	...	9,467	6.8	7.8	...	1,220	29 (1990)	28	...	39	38 (1990)	33
Georgia	20,046	5,325	4.7	4.6	4,261	1,154	27	34	37	24	36	42
Kazakhstan	...	59,422	15.6	15.6	...	3,814	27 (1992)	13	45 (1992)	27	29 (1992)	60
Kyrgyz Republic	3,788	2,613	4.1	4.6	931	565	34 (1990)	50	35 (1990)	18	31 (1990)	32
Pakistan	63,589	105,001	95.2	125.7	668	835	28	25	23	24	49	50
Tajikistan	6,454	2,138	4.7	5.9	1,376	365	33	39	40	32	27	29
Turkmenistan	9,506 (1987)	9,223	3.3	4.3	2,872 (1987)	2,161	27 (1987)	13	38 (1987)	69	35 (1987)	18
Uzbekistan	17,897 (1987)	16,875	18.6	23.2	960 (1987)	727	28 (1987)	26	38 (1987)	30	34 (1987)	43
East Asia	1,068,685	2,596,955	1,134.9	1,293.3	942	2,008	18	12	42	42	40	46
China, People's Rep. of	616,801	1,625,871	1,066.8	1,217.6	578	1,335	27	19	44	47	30	34
Hong Kong, China	79,674	140,520	5.5	6.4	14,422	21,835	0.4	0.1	30	15	69	85
Korea, Rep. of	257,792	590,829	41.2	45.5	6,255	12,978	11	5	37	38	52	57
Mongolia	3,507	3,428	2.0	2.3	1,775	1,480	19	41	28	25	53	34
Taipei,China	110,911	236,308	19.3	21.4	5,733	11,021	5	3	46	33	49	64
South Asia	430,882	742,648	929.0	1,141.2	464	651	30	27	25	26	44	47
Bangladesh	36,747	55,328	95.6	121.0	385	457	34	24	21	23	45	53
Bhutan	263	534	0.5	0.5	544	1,043	42	31	20	34	38	35
India	370,104	649,877	799.6	979.3	463	664	30	27	26	27	44	46
Maldives	...	...	0.2	0.3	...	...	11 (1995)	11	14 (1995)	13	75 (1995)	76
Nepal	5,602	9,083	17.1	21.9	328	415	51	42	16	23	33	36
Sri Lanka	18,166	27,825	16.1	18.2	1,130	1,528	27	23	27	27	46	51

continued.

Appendix Table A1.1. continued.

	GDP (2010 constant US$, million)		Population (million)		GDP per capita (2010 constant US$)		Agriculture (%)		Share in GDP — Industry (%)		Services (%)	
	1986	1996	1986	1996	1986	1996	1986	1996	1986	1996	1986	1996
Southeast Asia	**542,748**	**1,133,398**	**407.7**	**490.9**	**...**	**2,309**	**23**	**20**	**33**	**34**	**44**	**45**
Brunei Darussalam	9,302	11,528	0.2	0.3	40,547	38,115	2	1	59	56	39	43
Cambodia	...	3,857	8.0	11.0	...	350	47 (1993)	47	13 (1993)	16	40 (1993)	38
Indonesia	225,214	471,391	168.4	199.9	1,337	2,358	24	17	34	43	42	40
Lao PDR	1,672	2,840	3.8	5.0	442	572	61 (1989)	53	13 (1989)	21	26 (1989)	26
Malaysia	59,387	141,477	16.2	21.3	3,661	6,654	20	12	39	44	41	45
Myanmar	8,831	11,325	39.3	45.3	225	250	50	60	12	10	38	29
Philippines	77,566	111,364	55.8	71.4	1,390	1,559	24	21	35	32	41	47
Singapore	45,289	109,941	2.7	3.7	16,569	29,951	1	0.2	34	34	65	66
Thailand	91,515	221,897	53.0	59.9	1,727	3,706	16	9	33	37	51	54
Viet Nam	23,972	47,778	60.2	73.2	398	653	38	28	29	30	33	43
The Pacific	**...**	**12,208**	**6.1**	**7.6**	**...**	**1,822**	**30**	**29**	**27**	**30**	**43**	**42**
Cook Islands	...	...	0.0	0.0	...	...	14	10	11	7	75	83
Fiji	1,990	2,538	0.7	0.8	2,769	3,235	21	20	20	24	59	56
Kiribati	129	129	0.1	0.1	1,967	1,634	27	27	9	9	64	64
Marshall Islands	104	145	0.0	0.1	2,598	2,825	...	...	...	...	...	...
FSM	203	282	0.1	0.1	2,310	2,606	25 (1995)	25	7 (1995)	8	67 (1995)	68
Nauru	...	...	0.0	0.0	...	...	28 (1987)	7 (1994)	9 (1987)	14 (1994)	63 (1987)	79 (1994)
Palau	...	194	0.0	0.0	...	10,970	19 (1992)	4	13 (1992)	9	69 (1992)	87
Papua New Guinea	4,327	7,118	3.8	4.8	1,147	1,471	35	33	31	37	34	30
Samoa	395	439	0.2	0.2	2,463	2,564	23 (1994)	18	28 (1994)	27	49 (1994)	54
Solomon Islands	...	595	0.3	0.4	...	1,611	29 (1990)	41	5 (1990)	16	66 (1990)	43
Timor-Leste	...	...	0.7	0.9	...	...	...	...	...	...	...	...
Tonga	244	292	0.1	0.1	2,588	3,033	39	24	15	22	46	54
Tuvalu	...	23	0.0	0.0	...	2,528	18	25	17	11	65	64
Vanuatu	347	452	0.1	0.2	2,611	2,631	24	18	10	11	66	72
Developing Member Economies	**...**	**4,698,826**	**2,645.5**	**3,145.2**	**...**	**1,503**	**23**	**17**	**35**	**37**	**42**	**46**

... = data not available, 0.0 = magnitude is less than half of unit employed, FSM = Federated States of Micronesia, GDP = gross domestic product, Lao PDR = Lao People's Democratic Republic.
Notes: Where no data are available for the specific year headings, available data for the earliest and/or nearest years are reflected. Aggregates are provided for subregions/region where at least two-thirds of the economies and 80% of the total population are presented.
Sources: ADB. Statistical Database System. http://sdbs.adb.org (accessed 20 January 2017); World Bank. World Development Indicators Database. http://data.worldbank.org (accessed 20 January 2017); ADB estimates.

Appendix Table A1.2: Selected Trade and Social Indicators, 1986 and 1996

| | Trade Indicators | | | | Social Indicators | | | |
| | Exports (% of GDP) | | Imports (% of GDP) | | Life expectancy (years) | | Mortality, <5 (per 1,000 births) | |
	1986	1996	1986	1996	1986	1996	1986	1996
Central and West Asia	...	...	...	...	**61**	**62**	**133**	**115**
Afghanistan	...	...	...	...	46	54	209	149
Armenia	35 (1990)	23	46 (1990)	56	69	69	59	37
Azerbaijan	44 (1990)	30	39 (1990)	56	66	65	99	92
Georgia	42 (1987)	13	41 (1987)	32	70	70	50	43
Kazakhstan	74 (1992)	35	75 (1992)	36	69	64	58	52
Kyrgyz Republic	29 (1990)	31	50 (1990)	57	65	67	75	59
Pakistan	12	17	23	21	59	62	149	123
Tajikistan	35 (1988)	77	46 (1988)	80	63	63	118	116
Turkmenistan	39 (1991)	75	27 (1991)	75	62	63	100	89
Uzbekistan	29 (1990)	28	48 (1990)	34	67	66	81	69
East Asia	...	...	...	...	**68**	**70**	**53**	**44**
China, People's Rep. of	10	18	11	16	68	70	54	46
Hong Kong, China	109	136	100	138	77	80	...	...
Korea, Rep. of	33	26	28	29	69	74	9	5
Mongolia	30	36	81	42	59	61	130	80
Taipei,China	56	47	38	44	74 (1992)	75	...	...
South Asia	...	...	...	...	**56**	**61**	**143**	**105**
Bangladesh	5	10	12	16	56	63	168	109
Bhutan	18	35	52	46	49	57	159	100
India	5	10	7	11	56	61	141	105
Maldives	68	92	61	73	58	66	115	66
Nepal	12	23	20	36	51	59	170	102
Sri Lanka	24	35	35	44	69	69	27	20
Southeast Asia	...	...			**64**	**67**	**84**	**56**
Brunei Darussalam	62 (1989)	60	35 (1989)	61	72	74	14	10
Cambodia	...	25	...	44	52	56	120	123
Indonesia	20	26	20	26	62	65	100	64
Lao PDR	4	23	8	41	52	57	178	136
Malaysia	56	92	50	90	70	72	21	13
Myanmar	...	...	7	1	57	61	121	93
Philippines	26	41	22	49	64	66	72	44
Singapore	149	176	146	160	74	77	10	5
Thailand	26	39	24	45	69	70	46	27
Viet Nam	7	41	17	52	69	72	59	40

continued.

Appendix Table A1.2. continued.

	Trade Indicators				Social Indicators			
	Exports (% of GDP)		Imports (% of GDP)		Life expectancy (years)		Mortality, <5 (per 1,000 births)	
	1986	1996	1986	1996	1986	1996	1986	1996
The Pacific	...	...	...	...	**56**	**59**	**99**	**79**
Cook Islands	...	...	...	...	70 (1992)	71	27	21
Fiji	42	63	39	59	65	67	34	26
Kiribati	32	13	42	92	58	63	112	79
Marshall Islands	...	...	...	...	63 (1998)	67	59	42
FSM	3 (1983)	...	84 (1983)	...	66	67	59	56
Nauru	...	...	...	...	58 (1992)	59	57 (1990)	46
Palau	20 (1991)	13	...	67	67 (1990)	67	40	30
Papua New Guinea	44	59	51	48	55	58	96	82
Samoa	...	32	...	50	63	68	36	25
Solomon Islands	37	34	75	56	57	60	43	35
Timor-Leste	...	...	...	...	45	55	210	134
Tonga	26	20	70	58	69	70	25	19
Tuvalu	...	...	...	...	61	62	59	50
Vanuatu	35	46	65	53	62	66	45	30
Developing Member Economies	**22**	**36**	**23**	**37**	**63**	**66**	**101**	**82**

... = data not available, GDP = gross domestic product, FSM = Federated States of Micronesia, Lao PDR = Lao People's Democratic Republic.
Note: Where no data are available for the specific year headings, available data for the earliest and/or nearest years are reflected.
Sources: ADB. 2016. ADB Key Indicators 2016; ADB. Statistical Database System. http://sdbs.adb.org (accessed 20 January 2017); Directorate-General of Budget, Accounting and Statistics.http://eng.dgbas.gov.tw/mp.asp?mp=2 (accessed 8 November 2016); World Bank. World Development Indicators Database. http://data.worldbank.org (accessed 20 January 2017); United Nations Inter-agency Group for Child Mortality Estimation. http://www.childmortality.org (accessed 28 December 2016); ADB estimates.

Appendix Table A2.1: Loan and Technical Assistance Approvals, 1987–1996
($ million, %)

	Ordinary Capital Resources[a] ($ million)	Asian Development Fund[a] ($ million)	Technical Assistance[b] ($ million)	Total ($ million)	Percent[c]
Indonesia	8,579	735	90.40	9,404	21.40
China, People's Rep. of	6,346	–	100.03	6,446	14.67
India	6,338	–	34.57	6,372	14.50
Pakistan	2,334	3,434	44.01	5,813	13.23
Philippines	2,739	956	55.39	3,750	8.53
Bangladesh	3	2,997	47.24	3,047	6.93
Thailand	2,100	–	21.19	2,121	4.83
Sri Lanka	6	1,254	30.86	1,291	2.94
Viet Nam	30	937	37.72	1,005	2.29
Nepal	50	904	31.02	985	2.24
Malaysia	667	–	14.95	682	1.55
Lao PDR	–	574	37.34	612	1.39
Region[d]	241	–	155.26	396	0.90
Mongolia	–	315	28.70	344	0.78
Papua New Guinea	88	185	18.05	291	0.66
Cambodia	–	246	29.63	276	0.63
Korea, Rep. of	262	–	0.70	263	0.60
Kazakhstan	190	40	9.80	240	0.55
Kyrgyz Republic	–	160	10.67	171	0.39
Fiji	61	–	11.03	72	0.16
Uzbekistan	50	–	1.73	52	0.12
Samoa	–	40	7.70	47	0.11
Tonga	–	37	8.69	45	0.10
Marshall Islands	–	31	8.91	40	0.09
Maldives	–	31	6.46	37	0.08
Bhutan	–	27	9.87	37	0.08
Vanuatu	–	24	4.94	29	0.07
Cook Islands	–	21	5.70	27	0.06
Micronesia, Federated States of	–	17	7.64	25	0.06
Solomon Islands	–	15	4.99	19	0.04
Kiribati	–	2	4.30	6	0.01
Tuvalu	–	–	1.94	2	0.00
Myanmar	–	–	0.60	1	0.00
Afghanistan	–	–	0.10	0	0.00
Nauru	–	–	0.00	0	0.00
TOTAL	**30,082**	**12,981**	**882**	**43,945**	**100**

– = nil, Lao PDR = Lao People's Democratic Republic.
a   Lending operations include loan, grant, equity investment, and guarantee approvals.
b   Technical assistance operations cover grants funded by the Technical Assistance Special Fund and Japan Special Fund.
c   As percent of total lending and technical assistance operations.
d   "Region" refers to lending or technical assistance to a subregion or a group of member economies within the region, not to any particular economy.
Source: ADB loan, technical assistance, grant, and equity approvals database.

Appendix Table A2.2: Loan and Technical Assistance Approvals by Fund Source, 1987–1996

	1987	1988	1989	1990	1991	1992	1993	1994	1995	1996	%	%	Total
Total Lending[a] ($ million)	**2,466**	**3,135**	**3,691**	**4,008**	**4,771**	**5,114**	**5,230**	**3,728**	**5,585**	**5,335**	**100**	**100**	**43,063**
A. Ordinary Capital Resources	**1,509**	**2,051**	**2,328**	**2,528**	**3,424**	**3,960**	**3,933**	**2,551**	**4,130**	**3,669**	**70**	**100**	**30,082**
Indonesia	441	507	675	809	1,211	1,156	1,224	705	999	852	20	29	8,579
China, People's Rep. of	133	239	40	50	511	903	1,050	1,167	1,201	1,052	15	21	6,346
India	402	500	507	719	924	982	866	168	671	600	15	21	6,338
Philippines	44	207	423	461	177	266	310	68	531	254	6	9	2,739
Pakistan	250	331	343	337	410	3	20	145	160	337	5	8	2,334
All Others	240	268	341	153	191	650	463	299	569	574	9	12	3,747
B. Asian Development Fund	**958**	**1,083**	**1,363**	**1,480**	**1,347**	**1,154**	**1,298**	**1,177**	**1,455**	**1,666**	**30**	**100**	**12,981**
Pakistan	293	319	386	375	372	410	303	262	432	283	8	26	3,434
Bangladesh	266	268	338	356	419	256	331	280	227	256	7	23	2,997
Sri Lanka	106	108	127	196	198	120	84	130	140	44	3	10	1,254
Philippines	–	178	137	235	113	87	25	72	41	68	2	7	956
Viet Nam	–	–	–	–	–	–	262	140	233	303	2	7	937
All Others	293	211	375	319	246	281	293	293	382	711	8	26	3,403
Total TA[b] ($ thousand)	**25,971**	**45,915**	**68,342**	**83,075**	**84,742**	**92,761**	**103,457**	**106,752**	**133,476**	**137,631**	**100**[c]	**100**[d]	**882,122**
China, People's Rep. of	652	2,941	3,585	1,777	13,826	13,767	16,298	16,722	17,372	13,094	14	11	100,034
Indonesia	3,470	6,548	5,315	11,769	14,537	8,768	7,526	9,269	10,605	12,592	12	10	90,398
Philippines	1835	7,895	6,403	8,566	5,450	3,830	4,829	4,946	5,057	6,584	8	6	55,395
Bangladesh	479	1,950	3,227	7,967	4,905	8,059	6,983	4,349	3,586	5,735	6	5	47,240
Pakistan	2,863	4,449	6,551	3,759	5,230	4,545	4,065	4,805	2,855	4,890	6	5	44,012
All Others (including RETA)	16,672	22,132	43,261	49,237	40,794	53,792	63,756	66,661	94,001	94,735	54	62	545,042

– = nil, RETA = regional technical assistance, TA = technical assistance.
a   Lending operations include loan, grant, equity investment, and guarantee approvals.
b   Technical operations only cover grants funded by the TA Special Fund and the Japan Special Fund.
c   As percent of total TA operations excluding RETA.
d   As percent of total TA operations including RETA.
Notes: The top five recipients of Asian Development Fund, ordinary capital resources, and TA are listed in this table. Lending and TA approvals for all other developing member economies are classified as "All Others."
Source: ADB loan, technical assistance, grant, and equity approvals database.

Key ADB Milestones, 1987–1996

1987
- The Asian Development Bank (ADB) establishes an external panel led by Japan's former foreign minister, Saburo Okita, to conduct an in-depth study of ADB's role in the 1990s (completed in 1989)
- Framework of cooperation between ADB and nongovernment organizations is approved
- Revised policy on program lending (in support of sector policies and adjustment programs) is issued
- Disaster and emergency assistance policy with focus on Pacific countries is adopted
- ADB reorganizes its organizational structure, creating an environment unit
- Indonesia Resident Mission opens in Jakarta
- Board Committees rationalized: Audit and Budget Review Committees expanded from four to six members; Committee on Administrative Matters of the Board disbanded
- ADB reviews its income and liquidity policies along with loan charges

1988
- A Task Force on Poverty Alleviation convenes to formulate guidelines for ADB action and recommend directed and specific poverty-oriented projects
- A policy on education focusing on primary, nonformal, and environmental education is adopted
- ADB intensifies project administration efforts and introduces innovative and streamlined project administration procedures, e.g., delegation of more authority to executing agencies, earlier procurement and recruitment of consultants
- A new policy framework for guarantee operations that allows ADB to guarantee loans by private financial institutions to developing member countries (DMCs) is approved
- A comprehensive review of private sector operations is undertaken
- A policy on steamlining of technical assistance (TA) is issued
- The Japan Special Fund and Japan Scholarship Program are established by the Government of Japan
- The People's Republic of China and India are classified as Group A countries

1989
- Kimimasa Tarumizu becomes ADB's fifth President
- ADB launches the *Asian Development Outlook*, an annual publication series on the economic performance and prospects of the Bank's DMCs
- The Panel Report on the Role of ADB in the 1990s is issued, highlighting social infrastructure, living standards of the poorest groups, and protection of the environment as new priorities
- Private sector activities are reorganized within a new Private Sector Department
- A policy framework for speedy rehabilitation assistance to DMCs after natural disasters is designed
- The Environment Unit is upgraded to a division
- A primary education (girls) sector loan to Pakistan is approved, the first loan in which women are targeted exclusively as beneficiaries
- ADB opens the Pakistan Resident Mission in Islamabad and the Nepal Resident Mission in Kathmandu

1990
- The Marshall Islands and the Federated States of Micronesia join ADB
- A task force on strategic planning is established to examine ADB's strategic planning processes and institutional arrangements
- The Environment Division is upgraded to the Office of the Environment

1991
- Mongolia, Nauru, and Turkey join ADB
- The Strategic Planning Unit is established under the Office of the President to develop and coordinate ADB's strategic planning
- A high-level task force is appointed to recommend ADB's private sector operational activities
- ADB moves to its new headquarters in Mandaluyong City
- An administrative tribunal comprising three judges is established as an independent external and impartial appeal mechanism for the resolution of employment disputes
- The fifth replenishment of the Asian Development Fund and Technical Assistance Special Fund starts, and the Board of Governors passes the resolution in 1992 inviting members to make additional contributions

1992
- The first Medium-Term Strategic Framework, 1992–1995 is approved
- The Operational Program for 1992–1994 and 3-Year Rolling Work Plan with Budget Implications for 1993–1995 is developed
- ADB establishes the Greater Mekong Subregion program
- ADB resumes operations in Cambodia
- The Social Dimensions Unit is established to integrate cross-cutting social issues in ADB's operations
- The India Resident Mission opens in New Delhi
- ADB approves its first information technology strategy

1993
- Mitsuo Sato becomes ADB's sixth President
- Tuvalu joins ADB
- The Medium-Term Strategic Framework, 1993–1996 is formulated to establish a strategic planning process in ADB and sharpen country focus
- The 3-year Rolling Work Program and Budget Framework is introduced
- At the country level, country operational strategy studies are formulated
- The Guidelines for Incorporation of Social Dimensions in Bank Operations are issued
- ADB resumes lending in Viet Nam
- ADB reviews its major financial policies and currency management practices
- The *Human Resources Development and Management Operational Study* is completed

1994
- Kazakhstan and the Kyrgyz Republic join as members
- The fourth general capital increase (GCI IV) is approved
- The Medium-Term Strategic Framework, 1994–1997 is formulated to highlight the expanded role of operational agenda for ADB
- A policy on population is adopted, highlighting the relations between population growth and economic development
- The policy on the role of women in development (*Women in Development: Issues, Challenges and Strategies in Asia and the Pacific*) is updated
- *The Report of the Task Force on Improving Project Quality* recommends (i) further strengthening of project preparation, (ii) adopting stronger country focus, (iii) undertaking internal reorganization of ADB, (iv) emphasizing capacity building in DMCs, and (v) increasing beneficiary participation.
- The Confidentiality and Disclosure of Information, and the Information Policy of ADB endorse the presumption in favor of disclosure for a more open, accessible, and transparent organization—the first among multilateral development banks
- The Bank is reorganized to pursue better country focus (programs and projects)
- A new market-based window is established

1995
- The sixth replenishment of Asian Development Fund is started (effective 1997)
- Uzbekistan joins ADB
- ADB becomes the first multilateral organization to have a Board-approved governance policy that introduces the concept of sound development management
- ADB establishes an inspection function
- The policy on involuntary resettlement, which is designed to protect the rights of people affected by a project, is approved
- The policy on forestry is adopted, balancing production and conservation and encouraging participatory approaches
- The Strategy for Bank's Assistance to Private Sector Development is approved, highlighting sustainable investment in infrastructure and the financial sectors.
- The new energy sector policy is approved
- The new policy on agriculture and natural resources research is approved
- The Cofinancing Strategy and Review of Guarantee Operations is approved
- ADB establishes its first representative office in North America
- ADB creates its website, www.adb.org

1996
- Mitsuo Sato is reelected for a second term as ADB President
- ADB reviews its program lending policy, whereby sector analysis becomes a precondition for the modality, and poverty, social, environmental, and mitigation measures are emphasized
- A new sector development program is introduced
- The first loan for renewable energy (in India) is approved
- ADB revises its human resources strategy, focusing on the need to strengthen staff competencies, enhance work unit and staff productivity, and promote staff morale and professional growth
- The ADB Institute is established
- The European Representative Office and Japan Representative Office are established
- The Cambodia and Viet Nam Resident Missions are established

Note: Establishment dates of resident missions indicated above are dates of the host country agreements but if these are not available, establishment dates based on R-papers circulated/approved by the Board of Directors were used.

ADB's Organizational Structure, 1996

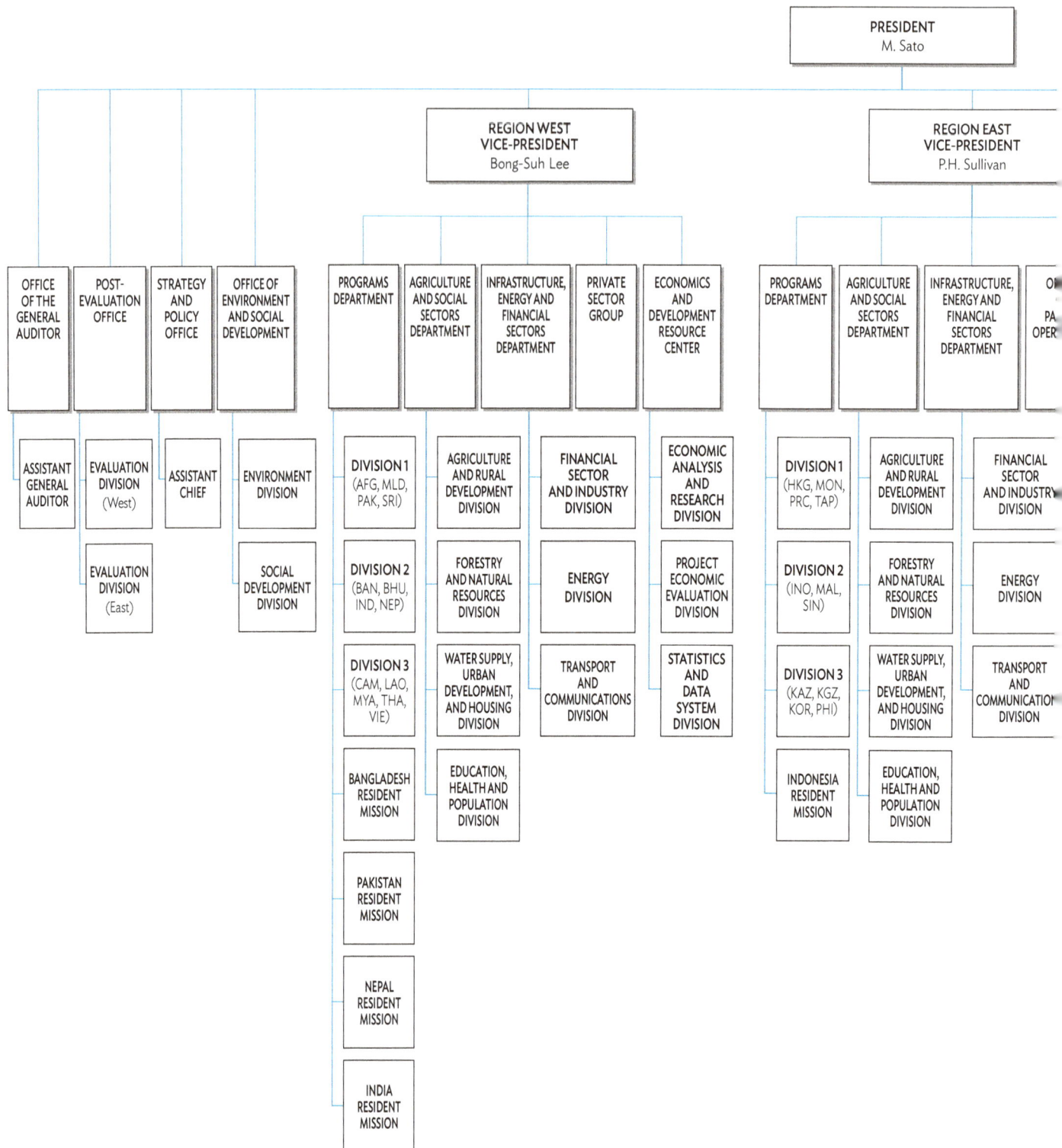

```
PRESIDENT
M. Sato
```

```
REGION WEST                          REGION EAST
VICE-PRESIDENT                       VICE-PRESIDENT
Bong-Suh Lee                         P.H. Sullivan
```

Region West Vice-President (Bong-Suh Lee) and central offices:

| OFFICE OF THE GENERAL AUDITOR | POST-EVALUATION OFFICE | STRATEGY AND POLICY OFFICE | OFFICE OF ENVIRONMENT AND SOCIAL DEVELOPMENT | PROGRAMS DEPARTMENT | AGRICULTURE AND SOCIAL SECTORS DEPARTMENT | INFRASTRUCTURE, ENERGY AND FINANCIAL SECTORS DEPARTMENT | PRIVATE SECTOR GROUP | ECONOMICS AND DEVELOPMENT RESOURCE CENTER |

- OFFICE OF THE GENERAL AUDITOR
  - ASSISTANT GENERAL AUDITOR
- POST-EVALUATION OFFICE
  - EVALUATION DIVISION (West)
  - EVALUATION DIVISION (East)
- STRATEGY AND POLICY OFFICE
  - ASSISTANT CHIEF
- OFFICE OF ENVIRONMENT AND SOCIAL DEVELOPMENT
  - ENVIRONMENT DIVISION
  - SOCIAL DEVELOPMENT DIVISION
- PROGRAMS DEPARTMENT
  - DIVISION 1 (AFG, MLD, PAK, SRI)
  - DIVISION 2 (BAN, BHU, IND, NEP)
  - DIVISION 3 (CAM, LAO, MYA, THA, VIE)
  - BANGLADESH RESIDENT MISSION
  - PAKISTAN RESIDENT MISSION
  - NEPAL RESIDENT MISSION
  - INDIA RESIDENT MISSION
- AGRICULTURE AND SOCIAL SECTORS DEPARTMENT
  - AGRICULTURE AND RURAL DEVELOPMENT DIVISION
  - FORESTRY AND NATURAL RESOURCES DIVISION
  - WATER SUPPLY, URBAN DEVELOPMENT, AND HOUSING DIVISION
  - EDUCATION, HEALTH AND POPULATION DIVISION
- INFRASTRUCTURE, ENERGY AND FINANCIAL SECTORS DEPARTMENT
  - FINANCIAL SECTOR AND INDUSTRY DIVISION
  - ENERGY DIVISION
  - TRANSPORT AND COMMUNICATIONS DIVISION
- ECONOMICS AND DEVELOPMENT RESOURCE CENTER
  - ECONOMIC ANALYSIS AND RESEARCH DIVISION
  - PROJECT ECONOMIC EVALUATION DIVISION
  - STATISTICS AND DATA SYSTEM DIVISION

Region East Vice-President (P.H. Sullivan):

| PROGRAMS DEPARTMENT | AGRICULTURE AND SOCIAL SECTORS DEPARTMENT | INFRASTRUCTURE, ENERGY AND FINANCIAL SECTORS DEPARTMENT | O... PA... OPER... |

- PROGRAMS DEPARTMENT
  - DIVISION 1 (HKG, MON, PRC, TAP)
  - DIVISION 2 (INO, MAL, SIN)
  - DIVISION 3 (KAZ, KGZ, KOR, PHI)
  - INDONESIA RESIDENT MISSION
- AGRICULTURE AND SOCIAL SECTORS DEPARTMENT
  - AGRICULTURE AND RURAL DEVELOPMENT DIVISION
  - FORESTRY AND NATURAL RESOURCES DIVISION
  - WATER SUPPLY, URBAN DEVELOPMENT, AND HOUSING DIVISION
  - EDUCATION, HEALTH AND POPULATION DIVISION
- INFRASTRUCTURE, ENERGY AND FINANCIAL SECTORS DEPARTMENT
  - FINANCIAL SECTOR AND INDUSTRY DIVISION
  - ENERGY DIVISION
  - TRANSPORT AND COMMUNICATIONS DIVISION

AFG = Afghanistan; BAN = Bangladesh; BHU = Bhutan; CAM = Cambodia; DMCs = developing member countries; HKG = Hong Kong, China; IND = India; INO = Indonesia; KOR = Republic of Korea; LAO PDR = Lao People's Democratic Republic; MAL = Malaysia; MLD = Maldives; MYA = Myanmar; NEP = Nepal; PAK = Pakistan; PHI = Philippines; PRC = People's Republic of China; SIN = Singapore; SRI = Sri Lanka; TAP = Taipei,China; THA = Thailand; VIE = Viet Nam.
Note: This organizational chart was as of 21 October 1996.
Source: Asian Development Bank.

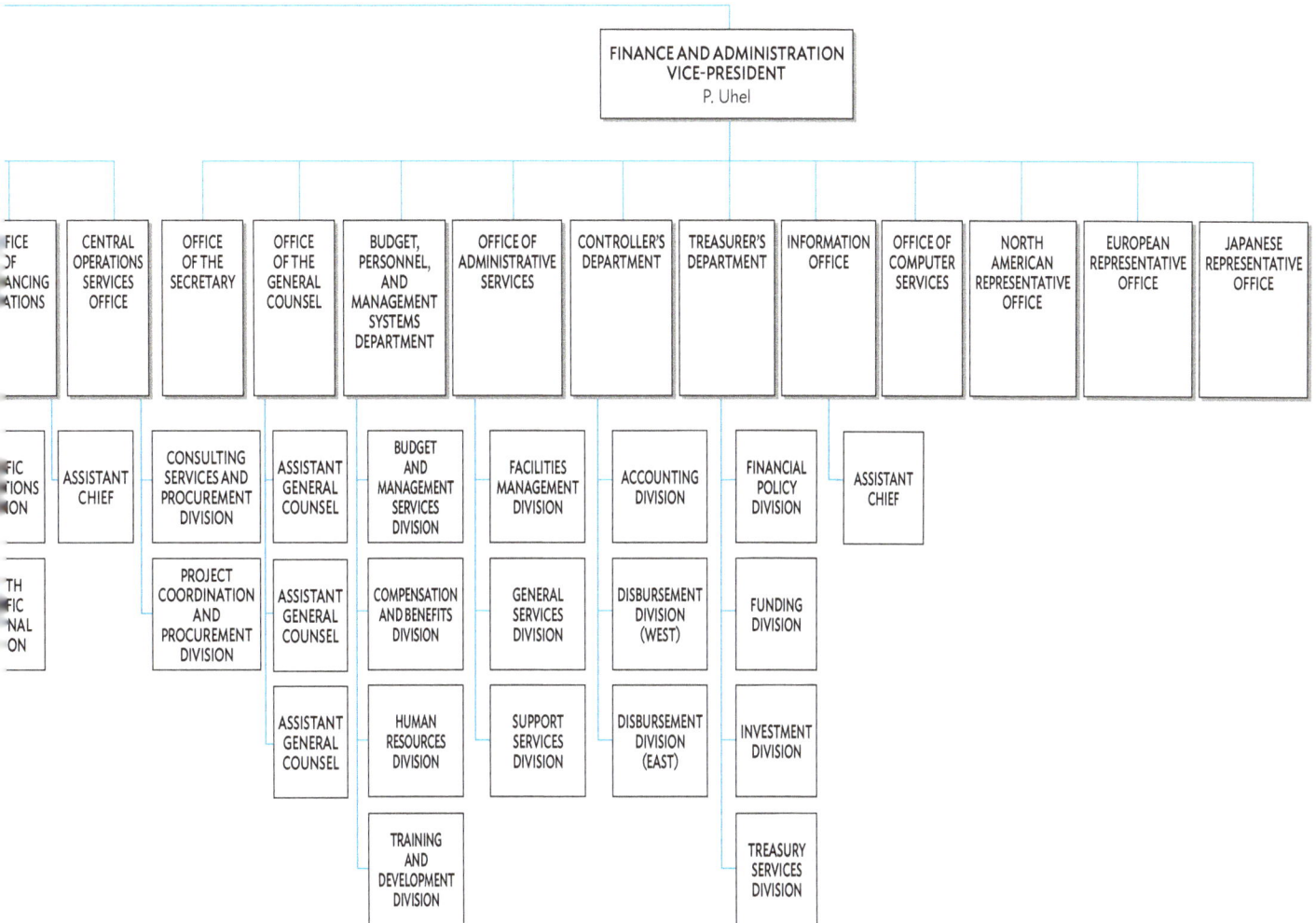

www.ingramcontent.com/pod-product-compliance
Lightning Source LLC
Chambersburg PA
CBHW061224270326
41927CB00025B/3494